CW00408985

Dr Paul Barnes is a Certified Accountant. He completed
his PhD at Sheffield University on the Financial
Performance of UK Building Societies and is now Senior
Lecturer in Accounting and Finance at the University
College of North Wales, Bangor.

  He is a member of Shelter and of the Building Societies'
Members Association and an active campaigner for
members' rights.

Paul Barnes

With a Foreword by Ken Weetch, MP

Building societies

The myth of mutuality

Pluto Press

London and Sydney

First published in 1984 by Pluto Press Limited,
The Works, 105a Torriano Avenue, London NW5 2RX
and Pluto Press Australia Limited, PO Box 199, Leichhardt,
New South Wales 2040, Australia

Cover designed by Mikki Rain

Photoset by A.K.M. Associates (U.K.) Ltd.,
Ajmal House, Hayes Road, Southall, Greater London.
Printed in Great Britain by Photobooks (Bristol) Limited

British Library Cataloguing in Publication Data

Barnes, Paul
  Building societies.
  1. Building and loan associations — Great Britain
  I. Title
  332.3'2'0941   HG2156.G75

ISBN 0-86104-759-1

To Sheila

Money is like muck: not good except it can be spread.

— Francis Bacon, 1612

Contents

Acknowledgements

The early research for this book was done for a Ph.D. at the University of Sheffield, where I was also a lecturer. I would particularly like to thank Professor Tony Lowe and Dr Colin Dodds (now at St. Mary's University, Nova Scotia), for their stimulation and guidance. I would also like to thank the trustees of the Houblon-Norman Trust for a most generous grant, which helped me enormously.

Even though he does not realize it, Alan Dobson, a senior producer at the BBC, was a great influence on my work. I am also very grateful to many other people for help with particular parts of the book. Firstly, to Chris Hendy who helped me collect the data that formed the basis of the statistical pieces. Secondly, to Nick Tarrant and Rob Gray who helped check part of chapter 8, and Hugh Davis who provided technical assistance. I would also like to thank Ronald Rowe at Companies House who made it possible for me to do company research even from such a remote place as Bangor. In this regard I would also like to thank Ken Weetch MP and his research assistant, Melanie Davis, and Dot Jones in Bangor for her reasonable interpretation of our library rules.

It is obvious that I would have been unable to write chapter 11 without the help of Christopher Punt, Chair of the Building Societies Members Association, and I am very grateful to him.

I would like to thank Jill Anker and Sue Potter for typing the manuscript under great adversity. I would like to thank Robin Chapman, Christopher Hird and Richard Kuper for their enormous help, by reading earlier drafts of the book and improving it throughout. Finally, I would like to thank, for their comments and information, those people in the building society world who would prefer to remain nameless, and the many others who would not wish to be associated with my views and conclusions. At times they all were quite inspirational.

Foreword
Ken Weetch, Labour MP for Ipswich

When ordinary people want to buy a house they encounter the big battalions; facing the buyer will be the institutions of the property market. These are interlinked by a chain of legally condoned restrictive practices and an extensive old-boy network. They will also represent, among other things, the social condescension of well-entrenched professionals who, whatever their shortcomings (usually many), are adept at duplicating work, spinning out time and knowing how to charge.

Underpinning the whole structure are the building societies. These have their origins in the self-help movement of the eighteenth century, from which many have grown into financial giants. Unfortunately, legislation and control over their power and activities have lagged behind their structural and financial growth. The net result has been the emergence of a movement that is far removed from the original objectives of being mutual institutions, being responsible to, and controlled in the interests of, their members.

Over the years the power and activity of building societies has been infrequently and only superficially debated in parliament. The latter, mesmerized by the uncritical and often orchestrated eulogy that surrounds the movement, has contented itself with ad hoc intervention, usually in line with short-term political expendiency. About fundamentals, too few critical questions have ever been asked, let alone answered. A number immediately spring to mind. Has the Building Society Association cartel had a beneficial effect for consumers? Has the feast-and-famine pattern of the supply of loanable funds had harmful effects on the construction industry? And while the lack of effective and meaningful competition between societies has led to the substitution of expensive and high-powered advertising of identical services, and a rash of branch offices on prime sites in our high streets, what line of official policy is proposed to deal with the oligopolistic financial giants that will shortly break the surface through prestige mergers? To these questions must be added a host of others which have come on the agenda since the Spalding Report suggested widening the legal range of building society activities.

The services of the housing market have long been organized to suit the professionals who sell them rather than the consumers, particularly working people, whose hard-earned savings buy them. This is sad, for the building societies could have used their financial clout to get expensive burdens off our backs. Perhaps, then, property valuations (the contents of which have only relatively recently been revealed to those who have paid for them) need not be duplicated. Conveyancing could become an in-house administrative practice rather than an expensive monopoly in return for solicitors' placed money. Who, however, could have expected anything better, given the self-perpetuating boards of directors – often composed of individuals with extensive property interests themselves – who have run the societies with an almost unbelievable lack of managerial talent?

There are a number of things that we have to get right. The first is the competitive position of building societies *vis à vis* other financial lenders who wish to compete in mortgage markets. Can we continue with features like the composite rate of income tax for building society investors? A decision has to be made regarding the mix of services that building societies are allowed to offer. Should they be allowed into estate agency, conveyancing and money transmission services in a major way? And, more importantly, should they enter high-risk areas such as insurance and banking? If the answer is yes, then a new and complex framework of regulations will have to be laid down.

It is quite clear, too, that building societies cannot continue masquerading as mutual institutions when their governing bodies move heaven and earth to prevent new talent being elected to the boards. If financial size and structural complexity dictate other forms of control, then these must be defined.

If Britain is to continue as a property-owning democracy, with its inhabitants becoming more mobile and home-ownership reaching further down the social scale, changes in building society practices are now inevitable and long overdue. Their activities must be sensitive and responsive to the needs of a wider social democracy.

A preliminary to this must be analysis, diagnosis and constructive prescription. All of these are provided in an intelligent and highly readable way by Paul Barnes in the following pages. I commend his work to you.

Introduction

This book presents the case for building society reform and for an end to the unacceptable aspects of their role within the housing system.

Chapter 1 outlines the criticisms that many groups have made of building societies' behaviour in recent years. *But such activities are merely the symptoms of a deeper crisis.* In this book I investigate the economic, social and motivational factors that have caused this crisis. Chapter 2 describes the legal and institutional framework in which building societies operate and explains the concept of mutuality. Chapter 3 describes the way in which the industry is dominated by five large societies and shows how funds are raised and distributed. A startling and disturbing picture emerges: with mortgage shortages, the poor and underprivileged lose out, and the wealthier and more secure benefit. Mutuality is shown to be a myth; housing finance is just like any other economic jungle in which the strong survive and the weak perish.

Chapters 4 and 5 discuss the motives of those who work in building societies: the economic objectives of building society decision-makers, the influence of the Building Societies Association, the role of building societies' boards of directors and local branch managers. Chapters 6 to 11 present these various motives in practice.

What is revealed is neither desirable nor does it accord with the public image of building societies. In these later chapters I challenge the virtue of the continuing trend for small building societies to be absorbed by the larger ones and question whether building society directors and their associates should use society funds for their own businesses.

Finally, in Chapter 12, in the light of the so-called death of the

BSA cartel, I discuss and make suggestions for reform – both on the most fundamental level and on the more specific aspects of the promised new Building Societies Act.

1. Official and consumer criticism

On a television chat show in May 1983 Clive Thornton, then Chief General Manager of the Abbey National Building Society, claimed that building societies were the 'highest form of socialism'. He meant that their sole purpose was to act as agents for transferring funds from savers to others wishing to buy their own homes. In fact, the original building societies were socialist in conception. They were associations of people in a particular town or village who lent money so that, one by one, each member of the association could borrow, to buy their own homes. These local societies have now largely disappeared. In their place are the multi-billion pound national organizations with all the usual trappings of modern big business: plush office blocks, boards of directors, professional managers and slick television advertising.

But as building societies have become big business, there has been a stream of public and official criticism of various aspects of their activities:

- building societies are a monopoly, maintaining an unnecessarily high interest rate;
- building societies discriminate against areas of our cities and people they don't like;
- building societies have cosy and corrupting relationships with various professionals involved in the housing market;
- building societies have more, and more luxurious, offices than they need;
- building societies are undemocratic.

High mortgage rates and a monopoly

As long ago as 1966 the Prices and Incomes Board said the

mortgage rate was fixed too high so that inefficient societies could survive and efficient ones make unnecessarily large profits.[1]

For many years building societies have operated a system whereby their trade association, the Building Societies Association (BSA) fixes (technically, 'recommends', or as they now say, 'advises') the interest rates they pay on deposits and charge on mortgages. In 1980 the Wilson Committee concluded that this cartel meant there was little incentive for most societies to keep their expenses below average and so led to waste.[2] The Wilson Committee was particularly critical of the unnecessarily large number of branches in certain locations, saying 'this must imply some waste of resources'.

To introduce some competition into the system the Wilson Committee advocated the abolition of the recommended interest rate. So did the National Consumer Council (NCC) a year later.[3] But the BSA made no attempt to break up the cartel.

The full implications of the operation of the cartel will be considered in chapter 4: whether the cartel is now dead, or whether the recent pronouncements to that effect are without any economic significance, but are merely political in the context of promised reform will also be discussed.

The shortage of funds

The Wilson Committee blamed the shortage of funds for house purchase from building societies on the operation of the cartel and the lack of competition between societies. Competition, it believed, could lead to reduced operating margins and higher rates to depositors. This would attract more funds into the building societies. The Wilson Committee also believed that the dismantling of the BSA recommended rate system – giving societies more freedom to compete with each other – would even out the flow of funds available for mortgages. At the moment the huge fluctuations in funds flowing into building societies – according to the prevailing economic conditions – means that at times mortgages are almost impossible to obtain and at other times (although rare) societies have surplus funds.

Chapter 4 will show that an *inevitable* result of the present system is a consistent shortage of mortgages, coupled with considerably fluctuating mortgage queues.

Discrimination

The existence of mortgage queues gives building society managers considerable power. Managers prefer to lend at the least possible risk, so are likely to be biased against people on a low income, ethnic minority groups, people of the 'wrong' sex or the 'wrong' sexual inclination, people who have uncertain health or job records, and people who want to buy in a 'bad' area. A mortgage queue gives the building society manager the opportunity to indulge such prejudices. There have been many instances of building societies discriminating unfairly against such groups.

In an article in the magazine *Roof* in 1976, Stuart Weir wrote:

> The evidence that building societies are starving older urban areas of mortgage funds is growing. They tend to regard older urban areas as unsafe places to use their investors' funds. There is . . . increasing evidence that they operate rigid and indefensible practices of red lining certain districts or even whole inner city areas. Red lining takes two forms: first, societies actually draw red (or blue) lines round certain neighbourhoods on the map and then virtually refuse to grant mortgages within these districts. Second, societies allow their view of certain neighbourhoods to transform their normally conservative policies towards old properties within them from a position of caution to extreme caution.[4]

Weir claimed that three national societies, the Leicester, Halifax and Britannia, had drawn a red line round the central area of Leicester. There is further evidence of non-lending on Birmingham's 'inner ring' of older areas. Weir also cited studies showing mortgage bans throughout the inner city of Leeds and red lining in Newcastle.

Members of ethnic minorities may be discriminated against, not only because they are poor, but because they belong to such a minority and have the skin colour or other mark to show it. Racial discrimination is a crime and no one is going to admit to it openly.

But in 1980 the *Building Societies Gazette* reported on the activities of one South London firm of estate agents which used a card-index system to distinguish between black and white prospective house-purchasers. Black applications were recorded on pink cards and white on white cards. Instructions such as 'no pink cards' would then be given for properties whose owners had said they did not want to sell to blacks.[5] The Commission for Racial Equality (CRE) has issued a non-discrimination notice to the firm in question.

In the late 1970s the BSA received a number of complaints that building societies discriminated against couples where the higher earner was the wife. A report was commissioned by the Equal Opportunities Commission in 1978 and this concluded that one in three building society branches would have discriminated in some way against such a couple.[6] The next year, a survey reported in the *Evening Standard* claimed 'either because they earn less than men, or because building societies look on them less favourably, women still buy cheaper homes than men.'[7]

Building societies also display hostility to single-parent families. One in every eight families in this country is headed by a single parent, and of these four-fifths are women.[8] The immediate problem facing a woman left with her children in the matrimonial home is paying the mortgage. According to the assistant director of the Child Poverty Action Group, there are three main problems. First, when the mortgage is in the husband's name, the building society sometimes refuses to negotiate with the wife, even refusing to accept mortgage repayments from her and thus allowing arrears to build up. Second, societies may give the newly single mother a short stay of grace to find a new home, rather than renegotiate the terms of her mortgage. Third, societies are reluctant to lend to a separated wife on a new mortgage because she is not judged a safe risk. In fact, the risk is often considerably reduced because in the large number of cases where single mothers are receiving supplementary benefit, mortgage interest payments are almost always met in full and can be paid directly to the society by the local DHSS office.

The NCC report[9] demonstrated how other groups – the elderly, the disabled and couples of the same sex – are heavily disadvantaged under the existing lending criteria.

Other than the red lining, building societies do not discriminate against particular groups in any direct way. But, given that mortgage funds are almost always heavily rationed, then the rule used by building society managers to allocate these funds will discriminate against underprivileged groups.

Relations with professionals

An important criticism of building societies is the part they play in the control of all the services connected with housing provision – planning, building, finance, and the sale of property – services which are provided by a set of interconnected professionals. The NCC cite a number of activities which are not in the interests of the consumer but which provide these professionals with monopoly profits.[10] This whole area is investigated in chapters 8 and 9 where the relationships between building societies, builders, estate agents and others in certain towns and cities are exposed.

The NCC report also criticized the agreements between local firms of solicitors, estate agents, other professionals and local building society branches. These professionals act as agents for the societies, providing them with funds from their clients, whom they are advising professionally. The amount of money raised for building societies in this way is considerable: professionals are generally paid commission, usually £1 per £100 invested. In many cases the clients are unaware that their 'advisers' have dual interests. In addition, professionals who invest in building societies are given favourable treatment for clients seeking mortgages. As the solicitor or other professional charges a fee for 'arranging' the mortgage, they are effectively being paid to help grateful borrowers jump the queue. However this only serves to increase the mortgage queue further and discriminates against the poor and ignorant.

Posh offices and poor housing

The monopoly profits of the building societies are, in part, diverted into wasteful management. The building societies are accused of having an unnecessarily large number of branch offices – the Orkney Islands have one branch per 660 people, Bournemouth one per 1,220. They are also accused of building grandiose head offices as monuments to their chief executives. The Britannia's new and magnificent head office is named Newton House after its chair, Sir Hubert Newton. Only a few miles away in the city of Stoke there are many homeless families and many derelict houses, partly due to the lending policies of most building societies.

Democracy

Many of these criticisms have been voiced by individual members of the building societies. Two of the most famous are Paul Twyman at the Anglia Building Society and Christopher Punt at the Nationwide. But their attempts to make the societies more open and accountable have frequently been rebuffed by the management. The issues and stories of these battles are told in chapters 6 and 11.

The concern of ordinary members about some of the practices and policies of their societies has led to the formation of the Building Societies Members Association with a membership of several hundred. There has also been much parliamentary interest, including full scale debate in the House of Lords in early 1983. And now the government has promised a new building society act. But, as later chapters show, it is likely to have serious weaknesses.

2. How the societies are run

The image of building societies as mutual organizations dedicated simply to helping people buy their homes, and highly regulated by the government is false. They are a self-administered cartel in which broader considerations of public policy have no legal force.

The constitution of building societies and mutuality

Building societies can be traced back to the late 1700s and the industrial revolution, when peasants came to the towns and cities for work in the new factories, and required housing. Faced with a lack of suitable accommodation in many new industrial centres, workers clubbed together to save for decent homes.

Most of these were 'terminating' societies, set up by a limited number of subscribers with the intention of providing each with a house over a period of between five and 15 years. Once this had been achieved, the society would terminate. Who received the first loans was decided either by who had made the first deposits, or by ballot or by competitive bidding – the latter method effectively determining the 'mortgage rate'.

Ideally a terminating society was a completely mutual organization; everyone contributed equally to its funds and everyone shared equally in the distribution of the society's assets when it terminated. The system had three basic weaknesses. First, as all members had to contribute equally it was difficult to attract new members after the society had been in existence for a year or two. To be on an equal footing with the founder members, late entrants had to pay back-subscriptions, and this was a burden. Second, if members had to depend on their own subscriptions to form the loan fund, then progress would be slow and some members would have to wait a long time for their advances.

The problem could be overcome. The fund could be increased, without increasing the demand for advances, by borrowing money from some investors who, instead of an advance, would receive a repayment when the society terminated. But this caused the third problem. If a sufficient amount was built up in the early years to satisfy all the demands for advances, then for the remainder of the society's life subscriptions would be flowing in, for which there would be no use. This problem was solved by arranging a ballot so that some investors could withdraw their funds with compound interest.

But such an arrangement was clearly unfair to those who were unsuccessful in the ballot, and so a further refinement was introduced: a new society was started. New members, discouraged from joining a society because of the large back subscriptions they would have to pay, could join the new society, which would borrow from the original society's surplus funds. The second society would then spawn a third society and so on. This arrangement was the forerunner of a 'permanent society'.

These permanent societies, developed during the 1840s and 1850s, had the 'additional virtue that while (the middle-class investor's) money was appreciating, it might also be helping to house the poor.'[1] But the permanent societies were also attractive to borrowers: they could repay their mortgage over a fixed term, confident in the knowledge that at the end of that period the house would be theirs, whether the society was successful or not.

But the permanent societies signed the death warrant of mutuality. By separating the borrower from the investor and insulating the borrower from the societies' success or failure, the investors – who bore the risk – regarded the society as 'theirs'. The growth of the permanent society considerably speeded up the growth of the investing building society member, and many at the time regarded permanent societies as the villains that were destroying the ideals of the small mutual societies. As the Royal Commission on Friendly and Benefit Building Societies said in 1871, when discussing permanent societies: 'It can no longer be said that the element of mutuality is essential to the type.'[2]

The word 'mutuality' appeared in neither the 1874 Act nor the 1962 Building Societies Act, which applies today. Clearly it was not the essence of a building society a century ago; it is even less so today when borrowers do not even have to join the mortgage queue and are not necessarily required to have been members. Nevertheless building societies claim to be mutual organizations and therefore different from, and more socially acceptable than other financial institutions.

But in fact, like banks, building societies are simply intermediaries between savers and borrowers. The only difference is that building societies, having no outside shareholders, do not distribute their profits. On this slim basis, they claim:

> The basic principles have remained unchanged over more than two hundred years and on this tried and proven foundation a 'grass roots' movement has developed into what many now call an 'industry' containing huge financial institutions.[3]

It is a purpose of this book to dispel the myth that the spirit of mutuality has remained.

The law

Building society law assumes the spirit of mutuality. Section 1 of the Building Societies Act 1962 states the purpose of a building society to be:

> that of raising, by subscriptions of the members, a stock or fund for making advances to members out of the funds of the society upon security by way of mortgages of freehold or leasehold estate.

Wurtzburg and Mills, authors of the authoritative book on building society law, write:

> that is all there is to it; and so it is that a building society is a society of a special kind, formed and regulated under particular Acts of Parliament for Special Purposes, and the rights and liabilities of its members depend upon the contract

into which they have entered, the terms of which are to be found in the rules of the society. A building society just cannot, either as principal or agent, do banking, insurance, or run unit trusts or anything else; its business simply is, being a building society.[4]

It is also easy to start a building society. Under the 1962 Act any number of persons, not being less than ten, may establish a building society, providing that each of them is willing to put £500 into the society, and to keep it there for five years. But, as Wurtzburg and Mills note, 'since this requirement came into force the number of new societies, excluding societies produced by unions, has been very small.'

But however simple it is to form a society, it is far from clear that the societies' members – those who provide the funds – have any control over the societies' policy. Day-to-day control is in the hands of the appointed managers, who are subject to the supervision of the Registrar of Friendly Societies. But when the Anglia Building Society's board wanted to merge with the Hastings & Thanet, the directors of both societies argued that members had no right to determine policy: there was a well-organized campaign against the merger by a substantial number of members.

The societies produced John Mills, the expert in building society law and joint author of the book cited above. As the subsequent report of the Chief Registrar of Friendly Societies says:

Mr Mills, on behalf of the societies, submitted that the members of a society have no right to interfere in those matters connected with the management of the society's affairs which under the society's rules fall within the powers conferred on the Board of Directors, and there is abundant authority to support him. He also argued that the investing members do not own the society, their rights being the right to interest on their shares coupled with their right to withdraw them.[5]

However, the registrar rejected Mills's arguments, concluding that building society members had 'the power to take steps to seek to influence the Board in the conduct of the society's affairs'.[6] Although the registrar said it was his 'prime function' to uphold and protect these rights, the law is ambiguous on the right of members to determine the policy of the society. The implications of a situation in which the owners of a business are possibly powerless in law are enormous and are a major concern of this book.

Government supervision of building societies

The Building Societies Act controls the operation of the societies, obliges them to publish annual accounts, restricts their borrowing and lending, and gives them certain privileges such as limiting the liability of members. It also regulates advertising for funds and the investment of surpluses.

The Act is administered by the Registry of Friendly Societies, whose job is to ensure that societies operate in the best interests of their members and the public at large. In practice, the chief registrar has considerable power. By law, the Registry scrutinizes societies' annual returns, which include detailed accounts. It can request information, conduct investigations and, with Treasury approval, prohibit or restrict societies advertising for new money. The chief registrar hears disputes involving building society law, authorizes mergers and takeovers, authorizes banks to hold building society money, and grants societies trustee status. But the powers of intervention and control go beyond this. Wurtzburg and Mills write:

> They [the chief registrar and the Central Office] have also a practical influence which extends beyond the formal limits of their statutory functions and powers. Thus, for example, if the Central Office makes criticisms and suggestions concerning particular proposed rules or suchlike, it is often better and more sensible to meet them than to fight them, although there is not in the Central Office any discretion or power to decline to register rules which in fact comply with the law; if the chief registrar in his Annual Report calls adverse attention to a particular business practice of which he disapproves, the practice is likely to cease.[7]

In 1981 a new government regulation, putting an EEC directive into effect, gave the chief registrar more power. Now building societies can only stay in business if they have been authorized to do so by the chief registrar. To get this authorization the building society has to have sufficient reserves and be run by individuals 'of sufficiently good repute and sufficiently experienced to perform their duties'.

Significantly, the legal constraints on building societies are primarily aimed at ensuring the soundness of societies as financial institutions. They are not concerned with the social and housing aspects of lending. In 1959 the State Building Society collapsed. Following this, new regulations were introduced aimed at controlling lending to property companies. These controls were inspired by concern about, and aimed to protect the financial stability of, the societies. They were not concerned with the social desirability of such loans.

Lending powers

A building society can only lend to members 'upon security by way of mortgage of freehold or leasehold estate'. (Section 1(1) of the 1962 Act) This means they can – and do – lend on offices, shops, hospitals, factories and simple land. They also lend on properties that are to be rented or held for speculation and money advanced on mortgages need not necessarily be used to purchase property. At times mortgages have been openly created or extended to finance holidays and the like. However this is now done more discreetly since a Bank of England directive in January 1982 warned that money lent on mortgages must be used only for house purchase or improvement, not for the purchase of consumer goods or to enable house owners to pocket capital profits on their homes. As *The Sunday Times* put it at the time:

> shrewd householders are remortgaging their properties with loans higher than necessary and spending the extra cash or investing it. They gain in two ways. The loan attracts tax relief, and the spare money can be invested at a premium on the mortgage repayment rate, even if this is a little over the normal 15% at present charged by building societies.[8]

There are other small restrictions on building society lending. A society may not provide a second mortgage unless they have also provided the first mortgage. And a society may not partially release a mortgage so that a first charge on the property may be given to others.

Building societies may not own property for sale or rental. They may not be directly involved in house building. However, the Abbey National has found a way round this by forming its own housing association and has obtained two of the Greater London Council's surplus house-building sites to build over 100 homes for sale and rent.

There are few restrictions on the adequacy of the security, the amount of the loan or the rate of interest charged. Each society decides this for itself.

Building societies can lend to housing societies and housing associations. They can lend to companies, though such lending must not exceed 10 per cent of the societies' funds. These 'special advances' are dealt with in detail in chapters 8 and 9. Building societies can, and often do, lend to their directors and staff and often at concessionary rates.

The BSA cartel

The practice of the BSA 'recommending' or 'advising' on the maximum share and mortgage interest rates was developed in the 1930s when competition between the societies was so intense that some faced financial ruin.

The recommendations are made by the BSA council, which consists of representatives from the 10 largest societies, the 10 regional associations affiliated to the BSA, 15 representatives elected from societies on a national basis, and up to four members co-opted by the council. All but 0.1 per cent of the funds in building societies are in the hands of members of the BSA.

Recently attempts have been made to underplay the importance of the BSA 'advice'. The secretary general of the BSA claimed[9] that half of the BSA members offered more than the recommended rate on shares, and more than a third were charging more than the basic rate recommended on mortgages. However, in practice it is very unusual for any of the large societies to step out of line – though some have done so for a short period – and most of the medium-sized and regional societies usually follow the recommendation. It is the numerous smaller societies that pay and charge the higher rates.

The way in which the rates are fixed makes it inevitable that building societies ration mortgages not by price but by a queue. The societies fix the share and mortgage rate so that the inflow of funds matches the outflow, as well as providing themselves with a margin for management expenses, tax and a small surplus to add to reserves. However, there is an in-built conflict. As they are anxious to make home ownership available to as many people as possible at the lowest possible cost, the societies are reluctant to set a high mortgage rate. But they cannot ignore competing interest rates from other savings media. The result is often that they eat into their margin by reducing the surplus they make. As this is small, in practice the cost-plus price for housing finance leads to mortgage rationing and periods of feast and famine. This is fully analysed in chapter 4.

3. Building society operations

This chapter explains the structure of the industry (dominated by a few big concerns), their lending policies (which favour the better-off), and their sources of deposits (largely the less well-off).

The structure

There are around 200 active building societies. As table 1 shows, at the beginning of 1983 the five largest accounted for just over half the movement's funds. The five largest societies are the Halifax, Abbey National, Nationwide, Leeds Permanent and the Woolwich.

Table 1

Total funds £ million	Number of societies	Percentage of total societies	Total assets £ million	Percentage of total assets
Over 3,500	5	2.2	40,665	55.7
£900–£3,500	11	4.8	20,323	27.8
£185–900	19	8.4	6,511	8.9
£45–£185	44	19.4	4,077	5.6
£2–45	94	41.4	1,437	2.0
Under £2	54	23.8	19	—
Total	227	100.0	73,033	100.0

Source: Building Society News, BSA, June 1983

Throughout this century, there has been a continuing decline in the number of societies. In 1890 there were 2,795; in 1979, fewer than 300. Until the early 1950s the decline in number was largely explained by the dissolution of terminating societies. Since then the number of takeovers and mergers has increased. Societies are in the last phase of a 30-year shift from the locally based friendly society to the national multi-billion pound societies.

The major increase in the concentration of funds has come through mergers and takeovers in the medium-sized societies. The largest five societies' share of funds has only increased from 50.1 per cent in 1970 to 55.7 per cent at the beginning of 1983. The industry's reorganization is illustrated by the rise of the regional societies – the Midshires, the Town and Country, the Gateway, for example – and the emergence of new countrywide societies such as the Anglia, the National & Provincial, and the Britannia. The Britannia, for example, is a collection of around 50 small societies coming together during the 1960s and 1970s. The Northern Rock is similar. Two new societies, the Midshires and the Town & Country, have been constructed as a conscious attempt to establish comprehensive regional networks. As Philip Court, chief general manager of the Midshires wrote of his society's policy:

> My board's thinking was that a completely restructured movement would emerge in the medium to longer term. This we felt could take the form of a two-tier structure. On one level, the number of societies operating nationally would be reduced to, say 10, with a nationwide branch network; and possibly a further twenty regional societies operating in strictly defined areas.[1]

More recently there have been mergers of large societies – such as the Burnley and the Provincial becoming the National & Provincial, and the absorption of the London & South of England by the Anglia – in an attempt to increase national branch coverage.

But whilst the number of societies has declined, deposits have grown hugely. Between the end of 1957 and the end of 1978 total funds of building societies grew sixteen-fold. As table 2 shows, for individuals they are the major source of borrowing and home for short-term savings.

Table 2   Personal-sector liquid savings,1982

	New savings		Amount at end of 1982	
	£ million	%	£ million	%
Building societies	10,059	57.1	66,758	47.5
Banks	4,037	23.0	51,709	36.8
National savings	3,519	20.0	21,672	15.4
Others	(26)	(0.1)	388	0.3
Total	17,589	100.0	140,527	100.0

Source: Building Society News, BSA, July 1983.

By the end of the 1970s lending by building societies to house-buyers exceeded lending by the banks to industrial and commercial companies.[2] The most notable effect of this growth has been the proliferation of building society branches: the takeover of the town high street by the building societies.[3] The number of branches began to increase fairly rapidly in the 1950s, it accelerated sharply in the 1960s and even more so in the 1970s. In 1955 there

Table 3   Distribution of branches, 1980

Size of society	No. of societies	No. with branches	No. of branches	Branches per £10 million assets	Branch staff per branch
5 largest	5	5	2,210	0.74	9.25
£600–£2,500m	12	12	2,012	1.39	4.68
£140–£600m	20	19	908	1.91	3.42
£35–£140m	48	42	489	1.43	3.20
£2–£35m	113	41	97	0.77	2.27
All	198	119	5,716	1.06	6.08

Source: M. Boleat, *The Building Society Industry*, Allen & Unwin 1982, p. 12

were 756 branches, today there are around 6,000. As table 3 shows, the medium-sized societies and the new regional societies have the most branches, relative to their size. This increases their operating costs and is discussed in chapters 6 and 7.

Building societies' role in the housing market

Undoubtedly building societies have played a major role in the growth of owner occupation in this country. The percentage of owner-occupied houses increased from 10.6 in 1914, 29.5 in 1950, 43.0 in 1961, 50.0 in 1970, 55.4 in 1980 to 58.0 in 1982.

For much of this time societies have lent less frequently on older housing than other types of property. They are also much more likely to refuse applications, or to offer low-percentage loans and shorter terms, on older property. According to Boddy building societies are likely to lend only 60 per cent of the value of poorer property, compared with 80 per cent of the value of sound, conventional post-1930 houses, even though the price of such property will reflect its marketability.[4] Building societies could consider the following as undesirable properties: very large houses showing signs of, or easily adaptable for, multi-occupation; houses with outside toilets, downstairs bathrooms, no garage or parking space, or lacking basic amenities; houses in urban areas with no front garden or forecourt which therefore open straight to the street; back-to-back houses and old (pre-1919) terraced flats; unusual or unconventionally constructed houses such as timber-framed or prefabs; and former council houses in areas still predominantly council-owned.

Even though the figures show a significant expansion of lending on older housing since 1975, Boddy concluded: 'a large proportion of the pre-1919 houses on which loans are granted are post-1900, societies remaining more reluctant to lend on nineteenth-century houses.'[5] Their preferences are aptly shown in table 4.

In addition, building societies prefer mortgagors with steady, assured and high incomes.[6] And table 5 shows that they lend proportionately more to the high income groups: 65 per cent of all buyers were paying over £20,000 for their house, at a time when the average house price was £23,644, and only 29 per cent of buyers

Table 4 The housing stock and building society loans, 1976

Type of dwelling	All houses	All owner-occupied houses	Houses owned-outright	Houses owned on mortgage	Building society loans
		Dwelling as percentage of total			
Detached	16	28	30	26	32
Semi-detached	33	37	30	42	33
Terraced	28	28	31	26	27
Purpose-built flat	15	3	3	3	6
Other flat/ rooms	7	3	4	2	2
Other	1	1	2	1	—
Total	100	100	100	100	100

Source: Building Society News, BSA, March 1983.

Table 5 Distribution of mortgages, 1982

Price of house	All buyers %	First-time buyers %	Former owner-occupiers %
	By house prices		
Under £14,000	20	33	5
£14,000–£19,999	25	32	16
£20,000–£25,999	23	22	24
£26,000–£31,999	13	8	20
£32,000 and over	19	4	36

Continued. . . .

Table 5 Continued . . .

By income of borrowers

Income p.a.	All buyers %	First-time buyers %	Former owner-occupiers %
Under £6,000	17	19	13
£6,000–£6,999	12	14	10
£7,000–£8,999	26	28	23
£9,000–£10,000	20	20	20
£10,000 and over	25	19	33

Source: *Building Society News*, March 1983

earning less than £7,000 a year when the average annual income was £7,540. Although it is clear that substantial numbers of people with below average incomes are helped by societies, it is equally clear that it is incorrect to characterize the societies as a movement which goes out of its way to help the mass of the working class.

For some time the local authorities filled the gaps of the building societies. Their lending was founded 'on helping those with housing needs who might not otherwise be provided for'.[7] For example, in 1974/5 an estimated 55 per cent of loans went to applicants wanting older property for improvement, 15 per cent to applicants who were homeless, 15 per cent to existing tenants and people high on waiting lists or displaced by slum clearance, and 8 per cent to staff urgently wanted by the local authority.[8] Proportionately more local authority mortgages were for older and cheaper houses and to lower income and age groups than building societies'; they also lent more generously in relation to house prices and incomes. But this support of the lower and more needy end of the mortgage market came to an end during the latter part of the 1970s and nowadays new local authority mortgages are rare. As table 6 shows, the major advance in mortgage lending has been by the banks, who do not serve the local authority clientele.

Table 6 Mortgage lending

Institution	End 1980 %	End 1981 %	End 1982 %
Building societies	82.1	79.1	75.1
Local authorities	7.0	6.3	5.9
Insurance companies	4.0	3.6	3.1
Savings banks	1.2	1.9	2.0
Banks	5.7	9.1	14.0

Source: Financial Statistics, HMSO.

In 1975 the government tried to negotiate a scheme whereby building societies would fill the gap left by the local authorities. Under the Support Lending Scheme, people could apply to a local authority for a loan and, if the authority considered that it would have granted a loan had funds been available, it would direct the applicant to a building society, which would treat the application in the usual way. Funds were set aside for the purpose. But the scheme did not work very well, primarily for administrative reasons. As the building societies did not believe that, as a result of the scheme, they were lending on properties and to individuals where they would not otherwise have done, few funds are put aside for it.

Of course, some societies have particular policies and schemes for certain groups. For example, since 1979 the Abbey National has been working with local authorities on programmes for Housing Action Areas. They have set aside significant portions of their funds for individual improvement and modernization schemes in certain specified inner-city areas. The newly formed Ecology Building Society has a distinct policy to lend on properties which, in the opinion of the board, are most likely to lead to the saving of non-renewable resources, the promotion of self-sufficiency in individuals or communities, or the most ecologically efficient use of land.[9]

Building societies in the savings market

Traditionally building societies rely heavily on the 'small' personal investor. It was estimated that, in 1977, 93.4 per cent of all accounts had less than £5,000 in them, and only 1.2 per cent had balances in excess of £10,000.[10] But considerable efforts have been made to attract the 'large' investor, as the insatiable demand for mortgages grew. During the 1970s, largely as a result of increased competition with others in the savings market, notably the clearing banks, societies started to offer investors more than the straightforward deposit accounts and shares.

Table 7   Distribution of building society savings

Type of account	Balance at end 1981		Balance at end 1982	
	£ million	%	£ million	%
Ordinary accounts	38,460	67.3	36,510	54.2
High interest accounts	5,610	9.8	11,400	16.9
Term accounts	9,840	17.2	15,790	23.4
Regular savings accounts	1,810	3.2	1,980	2.9
Other accounts	1,430	2.5	1,740	2.6
Total	57,150	100.0	67,420	100.0

Source: Building Societies in 1982, BSA.

A major development has been the 'term share', designed to tie up (and thereby stabilize) money seeking higher interest rates. In return for depositing money for a fixed period, the investors get a higher rate of interest, guaranteed to be a premium on the recommended rate on shares. Since their introduction in 1974 – when societies were desperately short of new deposits – term shares have developed so that now it is possible to invest for five years. Some societies have even offered six-year-term shares.

The significance of these developments is taken up in chapter 7.

More recently societies have developed less expensive forms of funds – notice or 'penalty' shares which usually pay one per cent more than ordinary shares in exchange for a penalty – generally a month's interest – on a withdrawal, or alternatively in exchange for three months' notice of withdrawal. Some of the large societies have also successfully started issuing certificates of deposits to limited companies and city institutions. It is thought that this will emerge as an important source of future building society funds.

Table 8   Savings by socio-economic group

| Savings medium | Socio-economic group % | | | | |
	AB	**C1**	**C2**	**DE**	**Total**
Building societies	19.9	30.7	29.1	20.3	100
Clearing bank current accounts	22.9	33.5	27.8	15.8	100
Clearing bank deposit/savings accounts	19.3	28.0	30.6	22.1	100
National Savings Bank accounts	14.6	25.1	32.0	28.4	100
Trustee Savings Bank accounts	7.1	20.9	37.6	34.5	100
Unit trusts	24.7	27.0	26.5	21.8	100
Stocks and shares	39.2	28.6	17.5	14.6	100
Life assurance	12.6	24.5	36.0	26.8	100
Total population	12.7	23.5	32.5	31.2	100

Note: The social grade classification is very broadly as follows: AB – upper middle and middle class; C1 – lower middle class; C2 – skilled working class; D – semi and unskilled working class; E – state pensioners, lowest grade manual.

Source: Evidence submitted by the Building Societies Association to the Committee to Review the Functions of Financial Institutions, BSA 1978.

As table 8 shows, certainly in numbers of depositors, building societies rely heavily on the C2 and DE socio-economic groups who account for almost exactly half societies' depositors. They are not a popular means of investment for the higher social groups, although they are supported by the lower middle classes, major beneficiaries of building society loans.

Building society taxation

Because they provide finance, building societies have for a long time enjoyed important privileges. These privileges extend to all aspects of their activities and have been a major factor in their expansion.

They pay corporation tax on their profits, but at a reduced rate of 40 per cent, compared with corporation tax of 52 per cent for most companies. The Wilson Committee recommended[11] that this concession – which was worth around £25 million in 1979/80, representing less than 0.2 per cent on the mortgage lending rate – be abolished. It still exists.

Mortgagors automatically receive tax relief on the mortgage interest they pay. No government has dared abolish this concession which costs the taxpayer around £15,000 million a year. The concession subsidizes house purchase and thereby makes it more attractive than other forms of housing. It has made borrowing by way of building society mortgage, whether actually for house purchase or not, advantageous over other forms of finance.

The sale of houses is exempt from capital gains tax. The Wilson Committee remarked that: 'This has undoubtedly both stimulated the demand for housing and, since the supply is unlikely to have been completely static, contributed to the rise in house prices.'[12]

Building society savers pay a low tax rate. The building society pays for the investor's tax on investment interest directly to the Inland Revenue. However the rate of tax is lower than the basic rate (30 per cent). The societies pay a composite rate of around 25 per cent. This rate is based on a sample of building society personal investors. As many building society investors are not liable to tax because of their low income, the average tax rate of building society investors is low.

Since the Inland Revenue lose no tax from these arrangements, *the composite rate acts as a subsidy from those whose incomes are too low to benefit from tax-free income to those who are taxed at the basic rate and above.* It has been estimated that about one in five people with building society savings are on very low incomes and are not liable to pay tax.[13]

As the Wilson Committee says:

> The effect of this arrangement is to enable building societies either to pay higher rates to their depositors than would otherwise be possible, thereby giving them a competitive advantage over other deposit-taking institutions, or to charge lower rates for mortgages thereby increasing the demand for them, or some combination of the two . . . Moreover we believe it to be wrong for non-tax paying society depositors, many of whom may be unaware of the true situation, to subsidize the taxpaying depositor or the house purchaser.[14]

According to the Wilson Committee, the only reason for the arrangement is administrative convenience. Both the Treasury and Inland Revenue are against the scheme in principle and Wilson recommended abandoning it. Nothing has been done.

It is clear that the tremendous growth of the building societies since the war has come from favourable taxation treatment and the desire of successive governments to encourage house ownership. After a decade of structural change, the building societies are now big business, dominating both the housing finance and personal savings markets. However their influence and policies are open to criticism. They are determined on grounds purely of financial expediency and they discriminate against the poor and needy. Despite the efforts by various groups, on the mortgages side, and by the societies, on the savings side, building societies tend to lend to the higher income groups and borrow from the lower.

4. Building society economics

The building society industry is characterized by price fixing (of interest rates), an absence of competition and domination by a few societies. This chapter shows how these features can be explained in conventional economic analysis and shows some of the undesirable effects.

Price fixing and stable interest rates

Chapter 2 explained how the BSA fixed the recommended (or, as BSA has called it since October 1983, the 'advised') mortgage and shares and deposits rates on a 'cost-plus' basis: acting together, the societies work out how much funds they want, fix the shares and deposits interest rate accordingly, add on the necessary amount to cover costs, and thus establish the mortgage interest rate.

What are the effects of this? Obviously the higher the interest rate offered to savers (especially relative to other investments) the larger the inflow of new funds. Similarly, the lower the mortgage rate, the greater the demand for new mortgages. But the building societies have to balance their inflows with their outflows of cash. If, for example, there is a big inflow of funds, what do the building societies do? They can lend all the money (increasing the supply of mortgages); they can cut the interest rate (reducing the supply); they can 'hoard' the money. In other words, there is more than one way of balancing inflows and outflows and these techniques can be used at many different levels of the flow of funds.[1] But, while the inflow can only really be fixed by interest rates offered, the outflow can be controlled by various means, the mortgage interest rate being just one. An alternative is rationing by queues and rules.

What would happen if the building societies tried to maximize their profits? First, they would be prepared to operate on a smaller margin if this increased the volume of funds and therefore the profit. So to some extent maximizing profits does not necessarily mean increasing the mortgage rate, nor does it mean reducing the rates offered to savers. Societies may prefer to go for slightly smaller margins, thereby increasing the flow of new funds, especially if economies of scale were available. However the room for manoeuvre is not great and margin-paring is unlikely to produce a massive inflow of funds. But overwhelmingly the evidence is that, if they so wished, building societies could charge a higher rate for their mortgages than they do and these funds would still be taken up by house buyers.

Building societies do not do this: they are not profit-maximizing and have an implied obligation to provide the maximum supply of mortgages at the minimum cost. So in practice they operate a cost-plus pricing system under which the mortgage rate is not fixed by demand but *by the amount of funds the societies themselves consider are required*.

The reasons for such a pricing policy are obvious. If building societies expanded their lending business they would attract mortgagors whom they consider more risky. Of course, as the societies claim, their business is fundamentally risky (borrowing short term, lending long), so there is some justification in restricting lending to the most secure borrowers and on the most marketable properties. The policy is even easier to justify publicly if it results in lower mortgage rates than would otherwise be the case. But by such a policy they control the mortgage and housing markets – to whom, and for what property, they lend.

Given the monopoly positions of building societies and their attitude to lending, profit maximizing could easily lead to more expensive mortgages, as the societies move to exploit their monopoly, and not necessarily to attract more funds. The present arrangement provides relatively cheap mortgages but tends to restrict them to the better-off. An alternative would be a more flexible mortgage rate structure, under which the risky and larger mortgages would attract higher rates. This would encourage societies to have a commitment to the individual borrower, instead of, as at present, to classes of borrower and property. Such a solution, while more socially just, would be difficult to achieve because it would remove building societies' monopoly powers. It would turn them into 'price takers' rather than 'price fixers'.

The building societies' ability to control the fate of many house buyers is almost wholly accepted by society today, because the detrimental aspects of monopoly power are assumed somehow not to result. Building societies are conventionally regarded as non-profit-making, benevolent, mutual organizations that would not exploit their positions. This is a serious misconception. The cost-plus cartel arrangement causes unnecessary mortgage queues and injustices that come from its administration. Instead we should move to a 'price minus' regime. That is, societies should fix the mortgage rate structure to satisfy as many house buyers as possible. From this the shares and deposits interest rate should be calculated. Such a change need not be so difficult, but there would have to be a radical revision in building societies' behaviour. This is the major objective of reform; its attainment is outlined in chapter 12.

Stable interest rates: the effects

Building societies have adopted an expressed policy of stable interest rates. That is, they try to minimize the changes in their own interest rates and attempt to 'ride out' any temporary changes in prevailing interest rates elsewhere. They say this policy is in the national interest. However there is no evidence that they are successful at it, or could be. Interest rates are determined by world markets, particularly USA. The UK, and certainly UK building societies, are price takers, whether they like it or not. Nor is there any obvious economic case for stable interest rates in preference to fluctuating interest rates.

Originally there was a valid case for stable interest rates. Building societies used to be faced with the huge task of recalculating mortgage repayments and so on, each time the interest rate changed. It was much better to change them only when forced to do so. The electronic computer has changed all this; it can perform such calculations in a moment. However, there is still a problem, as mortgagors and banks have to be notified of changes, but this problem could be overcome. The final repayment date could vary, or such fluctuations could be evened out in the terms of the mortgage.

The building societies' stubborn policy of stable interest rates has disastrous effects. It leads to feast and famine in mortgage lending. Reluctant to change their rates in periods of rising or falling interest rates elsewhere, the societies cause their own terms to lag behind. Building societies have the advantage relative to other competitors for funds (especially when the tax benefits are added) at times of falling and low interest rates. But, at times of rising and high interest rates, the terms offered by building societies will be competitively weak. So the funds that building societies attract will be highly volatile: large inflows at times of falling and low interest rates and small inflows at times of rising and high interest rates — with, of course, dreadful effects on the availability of mortgages. Admittedly, to a slight extent building societies mitigate the volatility by using their existing cash resources at times of extreme famine.

All this is shown in figure 1. The interest rate differential is a measure of the competitiveness of building society investments. The net inflow of funds follows the competitiveness. The liquidity ratio – the measure of building societies' funds held as cash – also follows this trend: when funds are scarce, societies use their cash reserves for mortgages.

The structure of the industry and competition

Chapter 3 showed that building societies dominate the mortgage market and the personal savings market, and that they are also given large privileges, making it difficult for others to compete with them. It was also shown that the building society industry is highly concentrated: the largest five societies have over half the movement's funds, the largest two (the Halifax and the Abbey National) with over a third of them. In economic terms these are classic oligopolies – a few firms dominating an industry. What is the effect of this?

Building societies' 'prices' are the interest rates they place on their mortgages and their savings accounts. They cannot determine

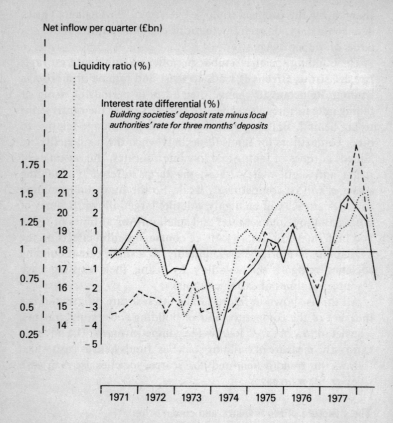

Net inflow per quarter (£bn)

Liquidity ratio (%)

Interest rate differential (%)
Building societies' deposit rate minus local
authorities' rate for three months' deposits

Figure 1 Net receipts, liquidity ratio and competitive position
Source: Lloyds Bank Review, January 1979

the inflows and outflows of funds in advance, even though these have to be balanced. All that building societies can do is determine the interest rates they offer on their products. (In a similar way most firms cannot determine the amount of goods they sell/make, they can only decide upon the prices they charge.) The economic theory of oligopoly helps considerably to explain building society behaviour.

The dilemma for oligopolists is how to extract monopoly profits from the near-monopolistic situation in which they find themselves. The problem is what the other firms in the industry will do. Each firm is reluctant to take measures which, when countered by others in the industry, would leave all firms worse off. Instead all firms attempt to set prices at the monopoly level. Chamberlain, a major contributor to the theory of oligopoly, writes:

> If each seeks his maximum profit rationally and intelligently, he will realise that when there are only two or a few sellers his own move has a considerable effect upon his competitors, and that this makes it idle to suppose that they will accept without retaliation the losses he forces upon them. Since the result of a cut by any one is inevitably to decrease his own profits, no one will cut, and although the sellers are entirely independent, the equilibrium result is the same as though there were a monopolistic agreement between them.[2]

No formal collusion or agreement is necessary. Each firm can make its own pricing decisions without prior consultation. Scherer writes:

> For the monopoly price to arise (and thereby produce monopoly profits) it is essential only that the firms *recognise* their mutual independence and their mutual interest in a high price.[3]

The basis of oligopolists' behaviour is their belief that their rivals will choose the most harmful of the alternatives available to them in response to a price change. That is, if a firm raises its price, rivals are expected not to follow suit, thereby enjoying an increase in the market share at the firm's expense. Or, if the firm reduced its price, rivals are expected to match the cut promptly in order to maintain their market shares.

Oligopolistic firms are not necessarily profit maximizers. The point is that an individual firm will expect any policy of 'going it alone' to fail and to damage its own prospects because the few but powerful other firms in the market will be able to exploit the change. It is a 'psychological' phenomenon if you like: the perceived reactions of others in the market to one's own price changes. Hence, in oligopolistic markets firms will try to avoid changing their prices, unless they are forced to. As Lowes and Sparkes say, 'price-changes tend to be infrequent, they tend to be rather larger than in other industries and furthermore, all oligopolists in an industry tend to change their prices at the same time – in response to some commonly experienced change, for example in wage-rates or material prices.'[4] Instead they compete in other ways.

A major point of oligopoly market analysis is that *firms will collude to fix prices – whether in some sort of formally constructed cartel, through an informal agreement in some smoke-filled room, or simply by a tacit agreement to follow the leader.* Adam Smith remarked that 'people of the same trade seldom meet together, even for merriment and diversion, but the conversation ends in a conspiracy against the public, or in some contrivance to raise prices.'[5] *What will not occur (or if it does steps will soon be taken to prevent it) is for oligopolists to compete – at least not in price.* In oligopolies non-price competition usually occurs: branded products, advertising and so on. In the UK this is seen in such industries as cigarettes and tobacco, breakfast cereals and washing powders.

The implications for an understanding of the building society industry are considerable. First, the BSA recommended, or 'advised', rate system is a cartel, which enables members to set prices (interest rates) for their own benefit. It may be going too far to say that it is designed to exploit a monopoly position, as in profit-maximizing, but it is similar. Even firms that do not seek to maximize profits – such as building societies — try to fix prices in order to prevent unnecessary competition, which would wipe out all the monopoly profits and benefits. It is evident to all of us that there is indirect competition: advertising, branch proliferation, branded goods (basically similar saving schemes but presented differently by different societies) and gimmicks. Perhaps the most important point is that *the undesirable aspects and effects of oligopoly prevalent in building society behaviour are inevitable, given the normal managerial/economic forces.* And changing this will only be achieved by the most fundamental attack on the nature and structure of the industry. The simple recommendation of the Wilson Committee, that the recommended rate system be abolished and competition be encouraged, is quite useless.[6] If there is not to be state control of the activities of building societies, the oligopoly, and more importantly the barriers to entry into the savings and mortgage industry, have to be broken down. These barriers are considerable: the tax benefits (other financial institutions find it difficult to offer such competitive rates) and the lack of incentive to move into the industry.

Because building societies do not have profit objectives, the incentive to enter is not as great as it is in other industries, particularly manufacturing industry. Additionally the rules for setting up as a building society, advertising for the first time and so on, make it very difficult. These factors no doubt explain why there have been so few new building societies. And the considerable tax privileges conferred on building societies explain why the banks quickly withdrew the assault that they had made on the mortgage market in the very early 1980s.

Product differentiation and price discrimination

A well known phenomenon of monopolies and oligopolies is the practice of splitting products into distinct sections in which different prices may be charged, thereby maximizing revenue and profit. Price discrimination can only be practised if the monopolist, or the oligopolists, can control their markets and prices; in particular, in segregating the various customer groups.[7] The electricity boards, for example, supply electricity to households at one price and to industrial consumers at another. The pricing activities of British Rail are quite remarkable in this respect, with the young and the elderly, for example, getting enormous concessions.

Price discrimination is only worthwhile if there are discernible groups of customers with different abilities to pay and/or different attitudes to prices and price changes. Firms are only able to maximize their profits by separating these different groups and charging them different prices. A policy of charging the same price for everyone has the effect of excluding certain groups unnecessarily and charging others prices less than those they would be prepared to pay if forced.

Consider British Rail. Two quite distinct groups of customers, in their ability to pay and reactions to prices, are business people and the elderly. The business traveller will be prepared to pay more and will be less sensitive to price changes. Most of their travelling is necessary and paid for by the company. The elderly person will not consider rail travel unless it is reasonably cheap, so British Rail offers various rail bargains to elderly people. The policy is extremely beneficial to British Rail as the cost of a few more people travelling on a train is very small. The effect is more revenue, fuller trains at little extra cost.

However business travellers may consider that there is a certain amount of injustice as they appear to be subsidizing the rail travel of elderly people and other groups. They may be especially resentful if they are paying more than they would if there were no price discrimination.

There are parallels with building societies. Building societies have to compete with other financial institutions, notably banks, for savings, and the 1970s proved a difficult period with the financial crisis of 1973/4, high rates of inflation and consistently high interest rates. The latter had a particularly significant effect. Until 1969 almost all societies' shares and deposits were in the form of money at short notice. As a result of competition from the banks, building societies extended their services to include contractual savings schemes (SAYE) and linked life assurance schemes. The most profound change occurred in 1974 when, in response to intense competition for funds, societies started issuing term shares for periods of between one and five years with a guaranteed differential rate over the basic share rate. Term shares were particularly popular as they substantially increased the flow of money into societies and incidentally increased capital stability. On the other hand this reduced margins, but all the larger societies, who were competing directly with the banks, adopted them.

Marketing people called such a policy 'product differentiation'. Doyle and Newbould write:

> Such a strategy recognises that consumers in any market are not homogeneous – that people do have different needs and expectations concerning a particular product. Such

heterogeneity is partly based upon differences in income, but it is also based upon socio-economic background, psychological factors and experience. This trend toward a strategy of differentiated marketing or market segmentation is reflected across a broad spectrum of business with firms offering multiple products and using multiple trade channels and media. Modern marketing recognises that it is rarely possible in today's competitive conditions to be all things to all people. Consequently, the competitive firm tries to increase sales by designing separate product and marketing programmes for each identifiable segment of the market.[8]

Various types of investors were identified. Two groups whose needs were not fully catered for were those who wanted to deposit their money for long periods, and those more sophisticated investors who moved their money around so as to obtain the best terms. Thus by offering different terms, the market could be divided and different prices charged (or rather paid) in order to maximize their interest. During the late seventies there were more product developments as further attempts were made to break down the market. The huge impact that the introduction of term shares had on new funds and the subsequent rise in the proportion of money raised in this way is probably the most significant event in building society history since the beginning of the 1970s. However not all of this is 'good news'. The term-share development had some frightening implications for the future. These will be considered in chapter 7.

Just as business travellers consider that they are subsidizing special age groups and others on British Rail, so may the ordinary shareholders/depositors consider that they are subsidizing the term shareholder. They are, and a monopoly allows them little choice – other than to become term shareholders themselves. But such a situation is rather unfair; the investor may need to withdraw some money before the term has expired. The societies are exploiting the ordinary investor's ignorance or inability to move money around the institutions to get the best return. Indeed, market discrimination is only worthwhile if customers have different abilities to pay or attitudes towards price changes. British

Rail adopted such a policy because they identified distinct groups with those differences. In a similar way price discrimination is only worthwhile while there are distinct groups of investors. More knowledgeable savers and those with large sums to invest are only prepared to invest if a society offers them terms at least as good as those available elsewhere. The ordinary shareholders are not so sensitive or knowledgeable as to the rates they could get with other 'products'. This may be 'loyalty' to the society (even knowingly altruistic) in the belief (justified or not) in its promotion of home ownership for all members of society. Other investors may believe (completely incorrectly) that they must invest with a building society for a long time before becoming eligible for mortgages.

Building societies and inflation

During a period of inflation building societies can become vehicles for shifting wealth from the less well-off to the well-off.

A building society mortgage, since it is a monetary debt, has a real value that falls with inflation because it is repaid in a depreciating currency. Investors' deposits will be eroded by the rate of inflation. Assuming that there are no other parties involved and no allocation of profits, any real gains by mortgagors will be matched by losses for building society investors.

The extent of this loss and gain can be seen by a comparison of BSA recommended rates on shares with the rate of inflation and house price rises in figure 2. Throughout the seventies, and for most of the fifties and sixties, inflation outstripped the interest rate to savers. Additionally the mortgage interest rate was less than the rate of increase in house prices and consistently so during the fifties and sixties. Harrington has shown that in no year between 1949 and 1969 was the real rate of return (mortgage interest rate minus inflation rate) greater than 2.39 per cent.[9]

How does this transfer show itself? For mortgages, the fixed monetary debt repaid in depreciating currency means that as inflation accumulates a smaller and smaller proportion of personal income is accounted for by the mortgage. This allows a larger part to be spent or accumulated in new savings. On the other hand, savers find that their capital is eroded and that they are effectively

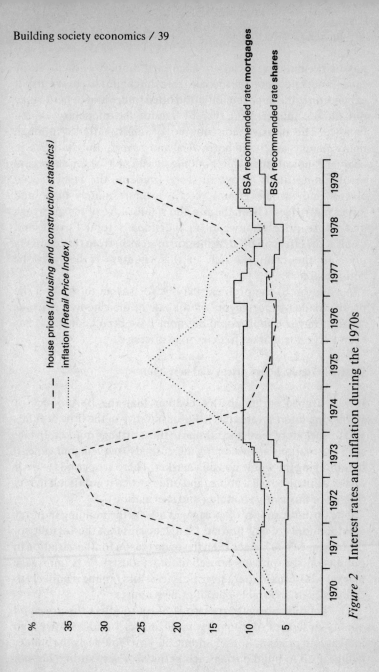

Figure 2 Interest rates and inflation during the 1970s

paying the building society to keep their money for them. If the saver is dependent on the income from the capital to cover current expenditure, the impact of inflation often forces him or her to take out all the interest and thereby reduce the monetary capital balance. This massive redistribution of funds matters. Although many people are both borrowers and savers, the statistics in chapter 3 indicate that while building societies have been successful in obtaining funds across all social grades – the higher social classes and income groups receive proportionately more and larger mortgages. Given the size and significance of the mortgage and house price relative to an individual's total finance and wealth, the effect on the distribution of wealth, from the relatively poor to the relatively rich in this country, is likely to be considerable.[10]

A solution to the problem may be for savers to share in the profits made by mortgagors on the sale of their houses. Various schemes have been proposed but none have been adopted. It has been left to the market to determine prices.

Unstable funds, house prices and new homes

It was argued earlier in this chapter that the BSA policy of stabilizing interest rates has led to instability in the flow of funds and to periods of feast and famine in the mortgage market. In fact such fluctuations are becoming increasingly frequent and violent, destabilizing the whole housing market. There are periods when it is very difficult to sell a house, and others when it is difficult to buy (these are times of gazumping and speculation).

The unstable supply of mortgages affects the building industry and the supply of new houses. Gough argues that the volatility of the mortgage market has been the main reason for the variation in output of the private housebuilding industry.[11] A mortgage market whose main characteristic is feast and famine is unlikely to create a high and stable output of new houses.

The volatile mortgage pattern is likely to affect the price and quality of houses. A comparison of figures 1 and 2 shows high increases in prices as housebuilding booms. Obviously the builder will gear up to build during such periods. A very strong, but not entirely unexpected relationship between the supply of building society money and house prices has been demonstrated by Gough.[12]

Final remarks

The major characteristic of the building society industry is that it dominates the markets in which it operates. It is ologopolistic and its behaviour is consistent with the usual predictions of economic theory. Building societies do not compete in prices; rather they fix prices that are mutually convenient, through the BSA. The BSA cartel by which interest rates are fixed by recommendations to members has been the main instrument by which the societies have exerted their monopolistic power. They have been duly criticized for this and disbanded it in favour of an 'advisory' arrangement (discussed in chapter 12). Building societies compete in indirect ways, such as by advertising and the use of branded goods. They adopt policies of price discrimination. In no way can these activities be seen as benefiting the consumer – nor can the activities of other industrial oligopolists. In a period of inflation, building societies have been instrumental in providing the house and property owner with large profits at the expense of the saver. In social terms this represents a shift of wealth from the poor to the rich. Attempting to minimize interest rate changes was shown to be a misguided and effectively divisive policy. As a direct result there were periods of feast and famine in the supply of mortgages. This caused considerable and unwarranted instability in the housing market and the building industry, thereby affecting house prices and the supply of new homes.

5. Managers' non-accountability

The previous chapter showed building societies operating in the mortgage and savings markets in their *own* interests rather than in the interests of existing and potential mortagors and savers generally. At first, such a conflict between the interests of the society and the interests of members seems incongruous, when one remembers that directors and managers are appointed to administer the affairs of the society for the benefit of their members (and that the Registrar of Friendly Societies is to supervize their activities in the interests of the community).

However, the separation of ownership from control is a well-known economic and sociological phenomenon and problem, recognized throughout the twentieth century. When firms were smaller the managers and shareholders were often the same people. Nowadays much private-sector industry comprises huge corporations whose directors and managers are quite separate from the owners. Their directors may not own one single share. In many cases such corporations are so large that no single shareholder or group can exert any influence on the company's decisions and policies. The latest development, of course, is the transnational corporation, which hops between nations and continents, apparently accountable to no one other than itself.

Both reason and casual evidence suggest that we should not expect the interests and motivations of shareholders and professional managers to coincide. If there is no group of shareholders large enough to exert some influence, then the firm will be managed in the interests of its managers rather than its so-called owners. There have been many studies investigating and validating this hypothesis.[1] There *are* constraints on managers. In the case of some major companies, large financial institutions, such as pension funds, hold big blocks of shares and can influence board decisions in a variety of ways. There is no such pressure on building societies. They have no large institutional shareholders. This chapter examines the effects of this separation of ownership and control on the running of building societies.

The consequences of managerial discretion

('Manager' is used throughout in the general sense, meaning anyone who manages, including directors. It is not confined to local branch managers.)

The importance of the discretion of managers in the operations of the large corporation has been widely recognized. Carl Kaysen has characterized the large corporation as one 'in which the constraints imposed by market forces are loose, and the scope for managerial choice is considerable,'[2] and R.A. Gordon has claimed that the development of the large corporation has led

> to a greater emphasis on the non-profit goals of interest
> groups other than the stockholders. Almost certainly, the
> personal and group goals of . . . executives are a part of the
> total value system – the desires for security, power, prestige,
> advancement within the organization, and so on . . . Profits
> are viewed as the basic constraint subject to which other goals
> can be followed.[3]

What motivates a manager and what influence does this have on the behaviour of the firm and its use of resources compared with other influences such as competition and the structure of shareholder power?

The motives of managers have been identified by organization theorists to include: salary, security, power, status, prestige and professional excellence. As it is rather difficult to measure these things, organization theorists have identified certain *activities* as measures of motivation. The theory of 'expense preference' is explained by Williamson:

> The essential notion that we propose in order to connect
> motives with behaviour is that of expense preference. That is,
> the management does not have a neutral attitude towards

costs. Directly or indirectly, certain classes of expenditure have positive values associated with them. In particular, staff expense, expenditures for emoluments, and funds available for discretionary investment have value additional to that which derives from their productivity.[4]

Profit acts as a constraint to this managerial behaviour, in that the financial market and the shareholders require a minimum profit to be paid out in such form as dividends. Otherwise the job security of managers is endangered. However, Williamson continues,

management will find it desirable to earn profits that exceed the acceptable level. For one thing, managers derive satisfaction from self-fulfillment and organizational achievement, and profits are one measure of this success. In addition, profits are a source of discretion (indeed, we define 'discretionary profits' as the difference between actual profits and minimum profits demanded). Discretionary profits represent a source of funds whose allocation may be importantly determined by managerial, in addition to economic, considerations. As with the expansion of staff, the expansion of physical plant and equipment provides general opportunities for managerial satisfaction and for much the same reasons.[5]

Managers' prestige, power and status are to a large extent reflected in the amount of indirect emoluments they receive in the form of expense accounts, luxurious offices, company cars, and others. These types of indirect emoluments have zero productivity: if removed, they would not cause the managers to leave the firm and seek employment elsewhere. They are discretionary expenditures, made possible because of the strategic planning that managers have in the running of the business. Indirect emoluments are probably less attractive than direct salary payments since there are restrictions in the way they may be spent. However, they may have tax advantages (since they are tax deductible by the firm) and they are less visible than salary, and hence less likely to attract attention and cause dissatisfaction of the shareholders or the labour force of the firm.

Finally, the status and power of managers is associated with their discretion in undertaking investments beyond those required for the normal operation of the firm. These minimum investment requirements are included in the minimum profit constraint together with the amount of profits required for a satisfactory dividend policy. Discretionary investment expenditure gives satisfaction to the managers because it allows them to pursue their favourite personal projects – an obvious measure of self-fulfillment for managers and top executives.

This view of 'discretionary' managerial behaviour also applies to regulated industries (and is therefore relevant to building societies). Of these Williamson says: 'the management of a regulated firm has an incentive to hold profits at or below some "safe" level by absorbing through expanding satisfaction-producing expenses.'[6]

In other words, in a regulated industry or one with a culture of 'no profit' there is an even greater incentive for managers to expand 'discretionary' spending. The theory of expense preference can be tested empirically, and the evidence will be considered later in this section.

A richer insight into this aspect of organizational behaviour is provided by Leibenstein's theory of 'X-inefficiency'.[7] This theory examines the *effort* exerted by *individuals* within the organization. Leibenstein's theory is that individuals determine their effort depending on the relationship between their own goals and those of the firm. They are unlikely to interpret and carry out their jobs simply in order to maximize the profits and productivity of the firm. Employees are presumed to have discretion and to be able to interpret their jobs to a greater or lesser extent. As this pervades the whole of the firm, maximum productivity is not obtained from those at any level within the firm. As a result, firms do not necessarily minimize costs nor make the best possible decisions. Leibenstein calls this X-inefficiency and it arises in the following contexts:

(1) A considerable amount may arise as a result of low pressure for performance from the environment. For example, there is no need for monopolists to minimize costs or strive for improved performance, since higher costs can be passed on to consumers.

(2) Even under competition, the pressures may be limited: the number of firms entering the industry may be small and without sufficient ability to produce at lower costs or offer better products than those already in the industry.

(3) Some firms may be sheltered either by a system of government regulation (for example, price regulation guaranteeing a 'satisfactory return' to all members of the BSA) or by situations in which firms operate on a cost-plus contract basis.

(4) Low pressure on firms to improve quality or reduce costs may exist because of inability by buyers of the services to understand the nature of the product. This may be true of many professional products such as taxation services by accountants, litigation services by lawyers, and prescriptions and diagnoses by medical practitioners. In all these cases the aura and mystique of the profession prohibits an evaluation by the customer of the quality of the services provided.

(5) Despite a reasonable degree of pressure from the environment, some firms may suffer from organizational deficiencies in communicating instructions and incentives through the hierarchy. Another and related cause for low performance may be that the wrong people are in the wrong jobs.

(6) There is no reason necessarily to expect firms to operate at minimum cost, even in an industry of many small firms, if the environment provides poor motivation for new ones to enter the industry.

So generally, X-inefficiency is caused by the way in which a firm is organized and how employees do their jobs. Although competition and other environmental pressures may lessen X-inefficiency, it is unlikely that the element of 'slack' within an organization would be eliminated entirely.

The evidence

Clearly, both Williamson's theories of managerial discretion and expense preference, and Leibenstein's theory of X-inefficiency apply to building societies. This is particularly so given that building societies are able to control their environment to a large extent through the BSA cartel, and face little pressure to minimize costs.

These ideas have been the subject of much research in the American Savings and Loans Associations (SLAs). SLAs are the US equivalents to UK building societies: some are 'mutual'; others are 'stock' or profit making. Verbrugge, Hillard and Davis compared the costs of a sample of mutuals with a sample of stock associations[8] and found that there was 'no support for the contention that mutual SLAs are less efficient than stock associations', and 'there is no evidence of X-inefficiency due to differences in forms of organisation'. In other words, variations in costs between SLAs was explained not by their formal objectives (profitmaking or non-profitmaking) but rather by environmental and other economic forces. More concentrated markets lead to higher average loan rates, lower deposit rates and a relatively smaller allocation of the total portfolio to loans.[9] In other words, when a few associations controlled the market, SLAs were able to take advantage of monopolistic positions to the detriment of their customers.

A similar study found the concentration of SLAs in a particular state was positively related to profit performance;[10] that is, the SLAs were able to extract monopoly profits in those states where they dominated the market, and this was appropriated in discretionary expenditure as suggested by Williamson.

So there seem to be common characteristics of oligopolistic/monopolistic behaviour of price fixing and discretion and X-inefficiency in the American SLAs markets. Chapter 4 demonstrated the behaviour of building societies in the UK. What evidence is there for managerial discretion and X-inefficiency?

This can be tested by examining building society operating costs. If building society managers exercised managerial discretion, operating costs (as a *percentage* of total assets) would tend to rise with the amount of profit. In my test, operating expenses were broken down according to the main classes and types of expenditure.[11] Some types of spending can be expected to be more discretionary than others, with different benefits accruing to managers. For example, the employment of more staff may provide top managers with larger empires and more attention. The use of unusually plush office accommodation would please them in a different way. Of course, some part of such expenditure is necessary; it is the excess — attributable to the excessive funds available for their payment — that is being interpreted as discretionary. The test was, therefore, whether particular types of expenditure significantly varied with society operating margins.[12] The types of expenditure were: staff remuneration, office accommodation costs, depreciation of offices, commission and agency costs, advertising, directors' salaries etc., audit fees, other expenses.

The results were that three of the eight variables varied with the operating margin. These were directors' salaries etc., auditor's remuneration and office accommodation, indicating that directors tend to pay themselves more if their societies are more profitable and that their auditors charge them more for their services and that the standard of office accommodation is higher. On the other hand the evidence suggests that the margin has no effect on the number of staff employed and the amount they are paid.

Branches

A major factor in building society operating costs is the number of branches, as the office accommodation factor mentioned above indicates. There has been public and official criticism of the proliferation of building society branches. Davies and Davies, who have meticulously counted them all, write of their home town:

> The main groups are within easy walking distance of each other. Thus, starting from the imposing head office of the Principality B.S. (which is next door to where this manuscript is being typed), a timed walk of less than two minutes brings one to the Bradford and Bingley B.S., next door to which is the Anglia, and in turn, next door but one is the very large frontage of the Halifax (one of its two Cardiff branches). Only three doors further on is the Provincial, also with a double frontage, while next door is one of the two Cardiff offices of the Glamorgan B.S. (the other is next door to the Cardiff offices of the Pontypridd B.S.). A large department store then interrupts the parade of building society offices before one reaches that of the Leeds Permanent. The result is

that the frontages of this half of St. John's Street, in the shadow of the 15th century church of that name, are dominated by building society offices. Again less than two minutes from the Bradford and Bingley B.S. is one of the two Woolwich branches, a few minutes from which is the Midshires, next door to which in turn is the Hibernian, with the Alliance four doors away (on the corner to the Cardiff Arms Park and next to the only T.S.B. branch in the city centre). Another minute brings one to the branch of the Bristol and West, almost opposite to which is the corner site of the Cheltenham and Gloucester; six doors further on we come to the main branch and administrative centre for Wales of Nationwide, opposite to which is the Abbey National's Queen Street Office, next door but one to which is the head office of the Cardiff Building Society . . . and so on for most of the 35 offices of the 24 societies which had full branch representatives in Cardiff in mid-1980.[13]

And how much does all this cost? Branching must be a discretionary aspect of building society activity. Some societies decide to set up branches with apparently scant regard to costs, while others manage without. For example, the Guardian, a medium-sized society with no branches, had operating costs of 39p per £100 total assets in 1979 while the Midshires, a society of similar funds but with many branches, had operating costs of 138p! Accordingly I investigated whether a society's branching policy determined its level of operating costs, again allowing for other factors.[14] It is by far the most important influence.

So there is evidence of discretionary expenditure. It takes the form of directors' salaries etc., but primarily of branching. That is, there are few profit constraints, most societies can afford to set up branches, irrespective of whether they are economic or not, and many do. It is just a matter of whether or not they wish to.

Do all building societies exercise their right of discretion and indiscriminately set up branches? Clearly not. Many of the very small societies cannot easily afford to do so and have no desire to either. All the large societies set up branches and the variability in their operating expenses no doubt reflects the relative efficiency of their branching operations. For example in 1982 two large societies had widely differing operating expenses: the Cheltenham & Gloucester had operating expenses of 76p and the Leicester of 125p per £100 total assets.

The medium-sized societies particularly show the effects of branching. Chapter 2 showed that one of the major developments in the last decade has been the development of the medium-sized societies with large and often regional branch networks. Table 9 shows how.

Table 9   Building society growth 1970-78

	'Big 5'	'Medium' — over £100 million	'Small' — all others	Total
Total assets[a] — £m				
1970	4,606	3,480	1,203	9,289
1978	21,489	14,278	3,771	39,538
Increase	367%	310%	213%	326%
Branches[b]				
1970	746 (37%)	1,041 (51%)	229 (11%)	2,016 (100%)
1978	1,799 (39%)	2,310 (50%)	486 (11%)	4,595 (100%)
Increase	141%	122%	112%	128%
Total assets per branch and head office[c] — £m				
1970	6,133	3,204	1,761	3,686
1978	11,912	6,099	4,923	8,051
Increase in assets ÷ increase in branches — £m	16,033	8,509	9,992	11,729

Notes: [a] Compiled from Registrar of Friendly Societies Annual Reports; [b] Source Davies and Davies;[15] [c] Counting head-office as one branch

Relative to their increase in total assets, the branches of the medium-sized societies have increased proportionately far more. The amount of funds relative to the number of branches is about half that for the very large societies. This difference increased during the 1970s, suggesting that the medium-sized societies' branches are under-used. (Comparison with the small societies should not be made as most of these have no branches.) Despite attempts to keep up with the very large societies, the medium-sized

Table 10 Operating expenses — pence per £100 assets

	Large	Medium	Small
1970	54.9	53.1	47.9
1978	83.9	100.8	76.7

Source: Barnes and Dodds[16]

societies' growth of funds was far lower. No doubt this accounts for the turn-around in costs.

At the beginning of the decade the medium-sized societies were relatively cost effective, compared with the very large ones, but by the end they were by far the most expensive. It should be noted that the small societies, many of which have no branches, are consistently the least costly. *These statistics in fact question the wisdom of branching.*

But can branching be justified in terms of growth? Surely the society that sets up the most branches will ultimately experience a greater growth of funds. Not necessarily. Small societies such as the Guardian and the Mornington have very high growth rates and can accommodate them by having large offices. I examined published data for the relationship between growth rates and operating expenses.[17] There was no correlation, suggesting that the costly policy of branching is unsuccessful. In fact the data suggested other reasons for growth success. The differences in individual societies' growth rates was accounted for by qualitative aspects: the locations of their branches (suggesting some optimal spread of branches across areas) and the timing of their new products, that is, schemes for investors. Societies that led the field in new products enjoyed much higher growth rates than those that tended to follow developments. Branching may be effective if properly planned. However, uneconomical branching is certainly unjustified when the secret of success lies in product developments.

Final remarks

This chapter has continued the theme of oligipoly of building society managers. As members have no effective control, managers have almost complete discretion in the running of their societies. This is nothing new in industrial organizations and, if they are operating in oligopolistic markets, the effect in many cases is a loss in efficiency and profitability. In the case of building societies (especially the medium-sized ones) it is particularly so with managers seeking the power and importance of the large societies by opening up new branches indiscriminately.

It is often claimed that savings in operating costs from increased efficiencies would have a negligible effect on mortgage interest rates. This may well be true. However, the unnecessary cluttering of the town high streets by building society branches demonstrates the absolute size of the problem. But there is a greater significance to the organizational behaviour explained in this chapter. In excess it may lead to financial disaster. We shall see why in chapter 7.

6. Growth through merger

For a long while now, it has been conventional wisdom throughout the building society movement to maintain that mergers are a 'good thing'. Such a view has been expounded by the Chief Registrar of Friendly Societies. For example, in 1970 he wrote:

> small societies are on average relatively more expensive to run than bigger societies. The majority are not yet of a size to be economic, fully independent units. Some will no doubt progress steadily year by year and will in due course develop in terms of size and standards of management . . . There are many others, however, where such ambitions are remote, where for one reason or another the future can only hold stagnation with consequential decline in status and relevance to modern life. Where there is no longer a worthwhile part to play, it may well be that the interests of members, and the building society movement in general, would be best served by a merger with another society.[1]

As the previous chapter showed, his opening statement ceased to be correct during the 1970s (see table 10). Nevertheless, 10 years later the view was maintained more adamantly:

> where there may be two or more small societies in one local area or within reasonable distance they should consider merging if thereby they may form a strong viable society better able to maintain that service. In a few cases this has happened, with good results; but I believe that for some small societies the time may soon be running out for this step to be taken with advantage.[2]

Such enthusiasm is reminiscent of the feeling about the large industrial conglomerates of the 1960s, that big is beautiful. The enthusiasm for conglomerate mergers was short-lived — not least because the results were disappointing. Nevertheless enthusiasm for large-scale building society mergers has remained high. For example, Phillip Court of the Midshires wrote of the decrease in the number of societies:

> But is the decrease rapid enough? I contend not . . . My society has actively campaigned for the Building Societies Association to make a study of the matter, but regrettably nothing has materialised, which causes me to express disappointment and concern, a view shared by others within the movement, who agree with me that if we cannot or will not put our house in order, there is a very grave risk that some outside agency will step in and do the job for us.[3]

The case for mergers surely cannot be as urgent as he suggests. Since that time his society has grown to be seventeenth in

Table 11 Comparison of Midshire's operating costs with the average for the movement (pence per £100 assets)

	Midshires	Movement
1978	125	98
1979	138	105
1980	153	116
1981	148	126
1982	182	129

Source: Building Societies Gazette and Registrar's Annual Reports

size. But at whose expense? His own society's operating costs have been consistently among the highest in the industry (see table 11). Further, it is not at all clear whether a society with many branches can be any 'better' than a society with only a few. Building societies, and building society branches, are very homogenous units. They offer two simple products: savings and mortgages.

A more plausible alternative explanation for merger and takeover activity can be seen in managerial motives. Many building society managers see takeovers and mergers as a more rapid means of extending the size of their societies than branching.

Maintenance of a generous profit level reduces the need to operate at minimum operating unit cost. Given that the BSA mark-up for mortgage interest rates has enabled even the most inefficient societies to cover their expenses, then a policy of mergers irrespective of cost is allowed to develop. Certainly the desire for increased efficiency is an unlikely motive. Even if such benefits were available, there is no guarantee that they would be obtained. Meeks, a major student of mergers in the UK, writes:

> A takeover which offered the *prospect* of higher profit, either through improved trading terms or lowest average costs for the combine, might in the event prompt not an improvement in profitability but a relaxation of effort on the part of the management or, in Leibenstein's terms, an increase in 'X-inefficiency'.[4]

Building society managers have been confronted by such criticisms of merger activity. Rather surprisingly, there was no vociferous objection. It was surprisingly well received by at least two senior building society executives approached for comment by Cooper.[5] They answered:

> There is keen competition between building societies to be the largest and most successful and many building society executives take pride in the success of their society and hope that this will be related to their own personal success. To expect anything else would be naive. (Name and society withheld by request.)

And, in perhaps more forthright terms:

> I am quite certain that the purposes of a building society as envisaged by its Board of Directors is to further the mutual benefit of investors and homebuyers but, human nature being what it is, the objectives of the chief executives of societies may well be to seek maximum growth in order that their own

power and influence and salaries shall also achieve maximum growth. This failing, if it is a failing, is equally true of limited companies. (Sir R.M. Chapman, Bt., FCA, Secretary, Shields Commercial Building Society)

The rash of mergers in recent years may be quite properly seen in the blind exhortations by the Chief Registrar of Friendly Societies and the pursuit of mergers by ambitious building society managers for their own ends of power and prestige, with no regard for operating efficiency. The rest of this chapter is given over to evidence concerning these alternative views. First we shall look at the movement as a whole and at the possible 'economic' benefits arising from merger; we shall then look at it from the members' or users' standpoint to find out what, if anything, they stand to gain.

The economics of mergers

The argument for mergers may be made simply in regard to operating costs. If economies of scale exist in an industry, then from a purely economic point of view mergers should be encouraged in order to achieve the lowest cost operating units. There is a widespread assumption that there are economies of scale throughout the building society industry, and that as a result mergers are a 'good thing'. The aggregate statistics do not necessarily bear this out (see table 12). The more notable feature is the considerable range of operating expenses unit costs within a particular size band. Given the absence of economic pressures to operate at minimum cost, the suggestion in the previous chapter of managerial discussion seems a much more likely explanation.

But are economies of scale to be expected, and how are they caused? Perhaps more importantly how may they be gained, and how may they be lost?

Building societies simply borrow and lend money. Usually 'they come to the public' through their branches. (But not always: a society such as the Mornington is mainly 'postal', advertising heavily, and with members transacting by post.) A large proportion of their operations are routine; some are carried out at branches, others at head office. A substantial part of building society work is

Table 12 Operating expenses of building societies by number within different size groups, 1978

Cost per £100 mean total assets	Size of total assets (£ million)				Total (of societies with over £2 million assets)
	Over 2,000	100– 2,000	25–100	2–25	
Over 115p	—	11	18	36	65
Over 105p up to 115p	—	11	4	13	28
Over 95p up to 105p	1	7	7	24	39
Over 85p up to 95p	4	1	7	14	26
Up to 85p	—	1	12	36	49
Total	5	31	48	123	207
Average (p per £100 of mean assets	90	109	103	102	98

Source: Chief Registrar of Friendly Societies Annual Report, 1978

therefore directly related to the number of customers and the amount of funds. The necessary co-ordinating and control that goes on in any large organization, together with the formation and execution of policies, is done at the head offices. This work may be largely unrelated to the volume of transactions or at least to changes in the number of them. Accordingly, we can see that potential sources of economies may come from:

• good and efficient co-ordination of procedures;
• effective and efficient locations and sizes of branches, in relation to the amount of business attracted;
• size, whereby those aspects of the society's work that are not related to volume, but have to be performed irrespective of variations of it, are spread over a larger amount of funds and customers thereby reducing unit operating costs;
• size, whereby a large volume of routine work is amenable to advanced mechanization, notably computerization.

These factors suggest that while there may be economies of scale especially for the very small societies (the last two items above), and there may even be diseconomies of very large scale, efficiency levels and unit operating costs are by no means wholly determined by size. On the contrary, how societies are run and organized are the motives, and 'effort' (in Leibenstein's terms) would seem to be more important.

Nevertheless, the existence of economies and diseconomies of scale is an empirical matter. What is the evidence? Unfortunately, it is not possible to know what is available, the data just tells us what has been achieved. Gough[6] concluded from data from individual building societies that there were no economies of scale, nor diseconomies. Gilchrist and Rothwell,[7] employees of the Halifax Building Society, claimed that there were economies of scale, but that they were only available to, and obtained by, the very largest societies.

Is merger activity consistent with a search for economies of scale? That is, are the types of societies that are actively involved in mergers those that would benefit from merger in increased efficiency, arising from operating on a larger scale? Alternatively, as suggested by Meeks, is merger activity more easily explained by managerial discretion and X-inefficiency? Table 13 would suggest

Table 13 Building society takeovers and mergers, 1970–79

Transferer[b]	Transferee[a]				
	Large	Medium	Small	Minute	Total
Large (top ten)	–	–	–	–	0
Medium (over £100m)	1	2	–	–	3
Small (over £10m)	3	7	14	–	24
Minute (under £10m)	25	53	54	48	180
Total	29	62	68	48	207

Notes: [a] Transferee, i.e. acquiring society, or remaining society in the case of a merger; [b] Transferer, i.e. acquired society.
Source: P.A. Barnes and J.C. Dodds[8]

the latter. By far the largest number of mergers involve small societies with small unit operating costs. Looking at these aggregate statistics there is little or no justification in economies of scale. In fact, our figures would suggest the opposite. Mergers between high-cost medium-sized societies have been rare.

But the case for mergers may not be based on such simplistic views of economies of scale. The data showing the huge range of unit operating costs suggests that at all levels there are very wide ranges of efficiency, in terms of efficient branch networks and other factors. There is, then, a very good case for mergers of inefficient societies of any size. Equally, there is a good case for the non-merger of the efficient ones, whatever their size. A merger may have a considerably detrimental effect on the first two types of potential economies of operation mentioned earlier. (Regarding the third and fourth sources listed, these may well have been fully obtained by all reasonably large societies.)

The case for mergers is therefore not simply one of economies of scale but rather the merits of the individual case. This even extends to the very smallest societies, many of which function on such a low level of unit operating costs as to be envied by even the largest societies.

The important point concerns managerial motivations and mergers, and the relatively efficient societies. Co-ordination and control, and the efficient running of routine operations may not be so easily or cheaply achieved. Anecdotal evidence of the merging of some large societies in recent years confirms that these can easily be lost. But the construction of an efficient and effective branch network (by far the major factor determining operating costs) is the critical consideration. The merging of large or regional societies causes duplicate branches and two head offices. The closure of overlapping branches in the interests of efficiency implies some loss of business; the closure of a head office is far more traumatic. Given the non-existence of economic pressures for cost minimization, and the forces at work suggested by Williamson and Leibenstein, it seems unlikely that the necessary reorganization following merger would come about. There may be efficiencies to be derived from many mergers, but there are powerful forces obstructing the realization of such savings. At the very least, merger proposals need to be fully considered and planned.

But are there merger benefits in practice, are these obtained, and are mergers carefully considered and planned? Again these are empirical questions. I examined the results of all mergers during the period 1970–78, other than those involving the very small moribund societies. In order to calculate the potential benefits (in terms of efficiencies) available from merger, I took the average operating expenses/total assets ratio for societies of a similar size to the acquiring society prior to merger, and compared it with a similar ratio for the same period for societies of a similar size to the acquiring society after the merger. I calculated the total received benefits from merger as the difference between the society's actual operating expenses ratio and the same ratio for the pre-merger size over the same period.

I inquired into three types of merger: all mergers, except those involving the very larger societies; takeovers of small societies by medium sized societies; mergers between small societies only.

Different types of merger occur for different reasons. I excluded the very large societies from my sample, as their acquisitions were of small societies where any merger effects would not be discernable. Most of them were 'cleaning up' exercises where, for one reason or another, the society had to be taken over, for example, Grays, Wakefield, following scandals. In the case of group two, the motivation is presumed to be the acquirer's desire to establish a larger and more comprehensive branch network. In the case of group three the intention is presumably to establish more economic and viable units.

Merger effects were calculated for up to nine years after acquisition. (Only in respect of the earlier mergers was there data for all the years.) The intention was to include as many years as possible since it was anticipated that merger benefits would not begin to occur until the medium term. Indeed, in the short term, costs may be expected to rise, due to reorganization.

The statistics showed that there were economies available from moving to the new organizational size.[9] However the results show quite clearly that these were not obtained. In fact, particularly during the early years, costs increased significantly.

In the case of small society mergers, the situation was not quite so bad. Here, available operating economies were not as considerable, although operating costs increased slightly. Again, they occurred in the first year, from the expected reorganization costs. In subsequent years they usually increased but not to a significant extent. In a way, the results are disappointing: savings would be expected to come more easily. The results for the medium-sized acquirers confirm the arguments made here: that a policy of acquisition, even though it could generate economies, would be far more difficult to achieve successfully. Costs were at a higher level than previously, even though they should have fallen.

There is another argument for mergers which may be tested in a similar way. The proponents of merger, and invariably the directors of the societies concerned, argue that members will benefit from a better range of products and an improved standard of service. If this is so, one would expect an increased growth of the society after merger, attracting extra members because it is offering more. Moreover, the previous chapter has provided some evidence that the very large societies experience a higher growth than others. Merger benefits — growth rate changes as a result of the merger — were calculated in a similar way to operating economies earlier.[10] There were enhanced growth prospects for merging firms as a result of moving to the new organizational size. However, the statistics indicate that generally they were not obtained.

A more significant growth effect may be expected from the merger of small societies. But the results for this group were very similar to the movement as a whole. It is with the medium-sized societies that we may expect improved growth rates since this is presumably the motivation for such mergers. (The societies in the sample merged frequently during 1970–78, showing a policy of expansion through acquisition.) The statistics showed that increased growth rates were to be expected in the early years, but that expectations were achieved in only some of the years under consideration. In other years the results were adverse indicating that there was no clear trend or result. On the whole therefore, this hypothesis of enhanced growth rates as a result of merger is not substantiated.

The developing structure of the industry, and the emerging new societies

The foregoing section dismissed the case for mergers on the grounds of simple economies of scale. In fact the reverse was true: that merger-active societies had higher operating costs, in both the short and long term.[11] The defence proffered by Court[12] — that we are still at a transitional stage before arriving at a 'two tier' structure — is both weak and alarming. Even in the long term (up to nine years) there were no palpable merger economies. But such a structure is almost impossible to achieve. The statistics suggest that only the five largest societies can achieve major economies of scale. The difference in size between the medium-sized societies and these top five show that, short of all societies merging

Table 14   The biggest building societies in Britain (by assets, £ billion), 31 December 1983 (or nearest accounting date)

Halifax	16.78	Britannia	2.38
Abbey National	14.31	Cheltenham & Gloucester	2.04
Nationwide	7.35	Bristol & West	1.57
Leeds Permanent	5.08	Yorkshire	1.21
Woolwich	4.85	Gateway	1.14
National & Provincial	3.92	Northern Rock	1.06
Anglia	3.64	Midshires	.68
Alliance	2.79	Town & Country	.64
Bradford & Bingley	2.69	Guardian	.57
Leicester	2.48	Coventry Economic	.57

together, such a policy of acquisition and merger is futile and untenable (see Table 14).

This, of course, means that the swamping of the high street by building society branches will not diminish with mergers. Quite the reverse. Mergers have not caused branch closures; it was never intended that they should. Any closure simply means the society has money for a new branch elsewhere, given the rise in the new medium-sized societies with ambitions for countrywide coverage. Today there are far more societies than ever before with a claim to a presence on every town high street.

The interests of members

Even though, on economic grounds, mergers may not be tenable, in practice they may be justified upon a closer inspection of individual mergers and the way in which members are affected.

There are two basic types of merger. The first involves two societies offering mortgage and investment rates in line with BSA advice. (We shall shortly be examining such a merger between the Anglia and the Hastings & Thanet). In the second type, one of the societies is offering rates above those advised by the BSA. Mergers of this sort are common, and usually involve small societies.

In the second type of merger, members of the society offering terms above those advised by the BSA are likely to suffer. The usual arrangement is that the new society will offer BSA recommended rates to savers, and that there may be some transitional arrangements or a bonus for those savers who previously received above BSA rates. Examples are the large London Goldhawk-South of England merger and the recent acquisition of the Severn by the Midshires. But it is not clear how mortgagors will fare in such mergers. The presumption that they will automatically pay the BSA advised rate (and therefore benefit from the merger) is not always correct. Many small societies offering above BSA terms take on 'high risk' mortgages involving special properties. In such cases, the new society may well argue that a rate over that advised by the BSA has to continue. But generally, savers with the acquired society will lose out and many mortgagors will gain. It is rather strange, therefore, that mergers have been accepted so readily by members, when savers outnumber mortgagors by a ratio of something like six to one. I know of only two cases in the last 20 years where members successfully voted against merger.

Perhaps there are other factors to account for the willingness of savers to accept mergers. Evidence for these comes from the press reports of some recent mergers. The Chief Registrar of Friendly

Societies was slightly critical of the conduct of the members' meetings to confirm the takeover of the Liverpool Building Society by the Midshires in 1982. According to a report in the *Building Societies Gazette*, he:

> hinted that societies should look closely at the way in which proposals for mergers are handled in the future. In particular, he pointed to the desirability of statements from society chairmen about the likely effects of the merger for the society and the members. He also expressed concern about the time and place of meetings which involve voting on special resolutions for mergers, and commented that societies could do more to hold meetings which gave the members the best chance of attending.[13]

Most of the questions concerned the loss of local identity, either the loss of the name, or the loss of yet another enterprise from Liverpool. Other questions were about potential redundancies in an area of high unemployment. The management gave reassurances on this. Voting on the special resolution showed a total of 7,080 members in favour of the merger, and 487 against. At the meeting itself, 97 members voted in favour with 29 against. There were also problems about the eligibility of certain members who had been allowed to vote. The registrar ruled however that the majority would have been affected very little.

The chief registrar also expressed partial criticism of the way in which the merger proposal was put forward and voted upon at the Cheshire-Accrington Savings and Building Society, a few months later. 'Some members,' he wrote, 'feared that the Board was attempting to force through the transfer at any cost, without regard to members' views.'[14] He also expressed concern over the receipt, custody and control of the proxy forms. A major issue at the meeting was compensation payments to some of the directors. Some members claimed that they were unnecessarily high. It was reported that:

> The Society's general manager and secretary, Mr Harold Hacking, receives £30,000 for loss of office from 30th November, 1982, the six directors who will lose office as a

result of the merger are to receive £45,000 divided between them, and Mr Alan Reeves, assistant general manager, receives £7,000 for loss of office. On a show of hands, about half those present at the hearing indicated that they would have no objection to the transfer proceeding if it were not for the compensation proposed. Others were concerned that the compensation and the 4% bonus to investors should be used to provide housing. However, they were assured that the reserves of a society are not available for this purpose.[15]

Again, the chief registrar came to the conclusion that 'the voting procedures were open to criticism, but he did not consider that, if the vote were taken again, the result would have been much different'.[16]

The acquisition of the small Stockport Mersey (£5 million) by the Bradford & Bingley was bitterly fought. At the members' meeting on 7 December 1982 to approve the 'transfer of engagements', voting was 436 for, 138 against. As the resolution required a three-quarters majority it was passed by a slender margin of six votes. It was then pointed out by a member that the Stockport board had infringed the constitution by giving 20 days rather than the necessary 21 days notice for the meeting. A new meeting was arranged for 24 March 1983. This had a considerable effect as members qualified to vote on a special resolution for merger are those who were also members at the end of the last financial year (Building Societies Act 1962, Section 69). E. Clouston in *The Guardian* takes up the story:

As the Stockport Mersey's last financial year ended on December 31, 1982, anyone recruited to the society in the few weeks between the date of the aborted meeting, December 7, and December 31 was qualified to vote at meetings in 1983. Hey ho ho.

In a letter to a member dated December 24, 1982, Mr Roberts said that between January 1 and December 22, the society gained 103 new members. Yet the total for the year, as announced in February had shot up remarkably to 350. This meant that in seven days, 247 people joined a building society already publicly written off, in effect, by its own directors.

People with a certain kind of nose smelled a rat. In 1980-1981 the Stockport Mersey had attracted nine recruits.

Inevitably suspicion falls on the Bradford and Bingley. They in turn stoutly deny any suggestion that they have been engaged in any co-ordinated (and technically legal) vote garnering among, say, the staff of their agencies.[17]

The major opponent of the merger, Mr K. Carroll, admitted that he was responsible for 'no more than 50' of the mysterious new members. For the board, the secretary attributes the increased membership to 'press interest'. In any event their financial investment was kept to a minimum. *The Guardian* article stated that well over 250 of the new members of the Stockport had invested only the required minimum of £1, and that they came from such places as Doncaster, Blackpool, Rochdale, Oldham, Stoke and Bingley.

The vote at the March meeting was as expected, 668 for and 126 against. Carroll's case was to a certain extent damaged when he was required to read out a public apology at the meeting, admitting that he had not complied with the chief registrar's ruling governing the content of his letter to members, which contained misleading information. Apparently this concerned a figure of £39,760 compensation. Carroll stated this was compensation for the directors when in fact it also included compensation to the assistant secretary.

The events demonstrate how the economic case for or against merger is soon forgotten in the heat of battle. It also exemplifies how the future of a small society may be left to the whim of the directors. Carroll argued, 'The directors have had enough,' claiming that the board even failed to acknowledge a marketing report his company provided. He cites the small but more ambitious Vernon Building Society in the same area, with a growth rate of 18.3 per cent for 1982 compared with the Stockport Mersey's 4.8 per cent, as an example of how the small society still is viable, given the will to carry on.

The registrar confirmed the transfer of engagements with no comment on the voting.

A recent merger in which a member questioned the benefits

involved the Paddington and its takeover of the Pecham Benefit. The member was Paul Twyman, a director of the Anglia and a member of the Paddington. One of his concerns was that his £150 deposit with the Paddington would earn one percentage point less after the merger than before. Twyman was invited to resign his membership after raising these matters with Mr T. Sutton-Mattocks whose legal firm acts as solicitors for the Paddington. When Twyman refused, he was expelled and his deposit returned. The Paddington was severely censured by the chief registrar in his 1981–2 report. He writes, 'The board subsequently told me that they had based their decision on hearsay evidence about the member, without giving him reasons or the right of reply. I regard both the reason and the procedure adopted in this case as totally inconsistent with the standard of conduct to be expected of the board of a member-based society.'[18]

Another merger strongly contested by some members was between the South of England and the London Goldhawk. A major objection was that larger building societies pay lower rates of interest. Their decision was defended by the management of the South of England, simply on the grounds that it needed to extend its branch network in order to provide a better service and so on. The major controversy of the merger however involved a payment of £10,000 to the auditors of the London Goldhawk who would not be auditors of the new society. Compensation for loss of office is sometimes paid to auditors under these circumstances in the building society industry although it is unheard of elsewhere. The chief registrar approved the merger but expressed reservations about the practice of these payments.

> Where on a transfer of engagements the services of the auditors are not retained, it is not unusual for *ex gratia* compensation for loss of office to be given under powers contained in the society's rules. Such payments cannot be condemned on legal grounds. But in my view when fixing the amount of that compensation the directors of the society should bear in mind that their primary duty is towards the society's members.[19]

Finally, my own society, the Severn, was recently taken over by the Midshires. The merger offered me a reduced rate of interest on my savings and the opportunity to use the Midshires branch network. Unfortunately they have no branches near where I live. Again there was an irregularity: members were not given sufficient advance notice of meetings to approve the merger and the chief registrar had to insist that it be reconvened.

From these few cases involving small societies (the less contentious mergers are not reported by the press, of course) it would appear that mergers are largely a formality in which the economic case for or against is hardly discussed. Inertia among members is considerable – far more than in the case of an industrial merger – and as a result their rights are not always treated as seriously as would otherwise be the case. No doubt also the choice of suitor by the directors of the acquired society will be influenced by the severance payments they are offered.

The most famous merger in recent years was the Anglia-Hastings & Thanet: a most acrimonious battle between the directors of the Hastings & Thanet and some dissenting members. Both societies were large with extensive branch networks: the Anglia had 120, the Hastings & Thanet, 92. The arguments in favour were:

> The elimination of the present development competition between the two societies. The increased status of the society if the present interests of both are merged. The existing preferential reserve ratio requirements available to a larger society. A greater potential for economy of management and development costs. A vastly improved national spread of branch offices and agencies for the benefit of existing and new members. Worthwhile opportunities for the co-ordination of computer, advertising and other specialist services. The similarity of the existing methods of operation and capital structure of the two societies.[20]

There was an 'overlap' in 19 places where both societies had branches. The societies said that in some of these the retention of both branches was justified but most 'overlaps' have now been closed. Nevertheless, the Registry of Friendly Societies accepted the argument that there would be reduced competition. (The registrar has to confirm a merger even though both sets of members have passed the necessary resolutions.) 'It seems to me,' he wrote, 'that scope for the rationalisation of the existing branch network may not be all that great but, apart from that, I think these are all valid points in favour of the merger.'[21] His concept of reduced competition involved branching. 'As things stand at present each society could be expected to continue to pursue its policy of branch expansion so that gradually the so-called "overlap" would increase.'[22] This is a strange argument, given that both societies were previously regional societies with comprehensive branch networks in their own areas. The merger made the Anglia a society with nearly national coverage. It had become one more society wishing to be countrywide with a branch in every town. Rather than eliminate the duplication, it has increased its number of branches at a higher rate than what would have been likely for the original societies. During the years 1979–82 it opened almost 100 new branches.

Although the merger was contested mainly on this issue, there were others. Some members complained about the compensation paid to the auditor who would no longer be employed. Several members cast doubts on the validity of the poll in the special resolution.

A major aspect of the merger meetings was the battle between the members opposing the merger, led by Paul Twyman, and the directors of the new society. Twyman claimed that his requests for information about the merger were 'brushed off' and that such treatment 'had a sinister connotation and was evidence of an intention to "steam roller" the proposals through.'[23] The chief registrar had some sympathy for Twyman:

> The impression I obtain from the correspondence is that Mr Twyman was for some reason assumed at the outset to be a member who could only cause trouble and obstruction, and for that reason it was thought unnecessary even to try to remove his doubts or to enlist his support. I believe that assumption and the society's reaction were both unjustified.[24]

The Anglia–Hastings & Thanet merger reflects the main characteristics of mergers contested by some of the members. The case for merger appears not to be rigorously examined (this is to be expected given the non-existent economic pressures on the decision) and that there is apathy from the vast majority of the societies' members – even though the merger may affect them considerably. When a few members question the merger, understandably the directors are caught off guard; the case for the merger is badly argued, voting arrangements are confused and the directors are offended when their autocracy is challenged and they are embarrassed. The major worry that the Anglia merger suggests for other mergers between large societies is how well thought out such mergers are. The Anglia board won no intellectual battles. (Their argument about preferential reserve ratio requirements being available to a large society is nonsense. Neither the Anglia nor the Hastings & Thanet was near the statutory minimum and this could only be achieved by making heavy losses over many years.) The new society operates with, effectively, two large head offices and there have been reports of alleged problems concerning the compatibility of the two computing and data processing functions. The Anglia has now merged with another large society, the London & South of England. This society has a large head office near London and 32 of its branches are in similar districts and towns to the Anglia (17 have been closed and the remainder kept in operation, at least for the medium term). This merger engendered less hostility: Paul Twyman had been invited to the board of the new society.

Final remarks

Mergers are a major aspect of the new building societies industry. Over the last few decades more than one small building society a month has been disappearing, with scarcely a newspaper line to record the event. Does it matter? Who cares? The evidence presented here suggests that it *does* matter. There is no economic justification for the merger mania that has gone on in the industry for many years, encouraged by the chief registrar. The study of the results of mergers shows quite unequivocally that while there may have been economies they were almost never achieved. The explanation for merger mania lies not in desire for efficiency but rather in the prestige and status sought by those who want to run very large societies.

But the case against mergers is not a narrow economic one. In addition to offering above BSA rates, many small societies play an important social role, and lend on property that the larger societies would not usually consider. The Ecology Building Society has already been mentioned; the Catholic and the Teachers are others with specified social obligations regarding their mortgage advances. The Mornington and the St Pancras have fulfilled a major social role in North London housing, lending on properties and concentrating on areas usually avoided by the larger societies. Unfortunately, the case against mergers, and especially those involving the absorption of small societies is weakened enormously while societies' lending policies and practices are not published. If the details of these were quantified then the important qualitative effects of mergers on housing would be known and understood.

While there is inadequate information it is likely that few will care about the consequences of mergers. This surely is undesirable; many societies will be taken over when it would have been better that they continued. In this atmosphere of ignorance, the merger-happy barons of the building society world will continue to achieve their needs by dismissing the few dissenting members and embarking on mergers, the social and economic consequences of which are either not considered or cast aside.

7. Accounting practices

In earlier chapters it was argued that managerial motives were not necessarily consistent with members' wishes, mainly in expense preference and the proliferation of unnecessary branches. Here we discuss another aspect: the creation of forms of savings that are very costly to societies, and ask what happens if excessive amounts of these two are combined.

Loss-making products: term shares

The financial crisis of the early 1970s had a profound effect on building societies, when the banks attempted to offer far more competitive terms to savers. Building societies reacted sharply by extending their services to include contractual savings schemes, linked life assurance and other schemes. The most important development was the term share, whereby a guaranteed differential rate was paid over the basis share rate on deposits with the society for fixed periods. These were popular, substantially increasing the flow of money into societies. Throughout much of the remainder of the decade, both inflation and interest rates were exceptionally high and, if societies were to maintain their competitive position with regard to the banks, they had to continue to offer these higher cost products. They also had to maintain existing funds. Accordingly the terms were lengthened from one or two years, in the first instance, to five or even six years (see table 15). Usually, one-year term shares offered an extra $\frac{1}{2}$ per cent on BSA recommended rates for ordinary shares, two-year term shares an extra 1 per cent and so on. Societies also started offering open-ended term shares whereby a premium, usually of 2 per cent over the ordinary share rate for a five-year term, was paid and the

Table 15 The growth of term shares

	Term share as a % of total funds	Length of term share as a % of total term shares			
		2 yrs	3 yrs	4 yrs	5 yrs
1978	10.6	25.4	63.7	____10.1____	
1979	13.4	14.8	48.1	17.9	17.7
1980	14.7	3.5	30.2	13.8	41.2
1981	17.2	n/a	n/a	n/a	n/a
1982	23.4	n/a	n/a	n/a	n/a

n/a: No longer made available by the BSA
Source: BSA

money left to continue earning that higher rate, but only subject to three months notice of withdrawal.

The problem with term shares is their effect upon margins, societies' increasing dependence upon them, and the inevitable drift towards longer terms. Some societies were opposed from the start to term shares and were concerned about where such a development might lead. For example, the Bristol & West and the Burnley avoided them though other societies of similar sizes embraced the development. The trend towards longer terms has deep implications. Longer term shares are gross loss-makers. For example in late 1981 and early 1982 the mortgage rate was 13 per cent, the ordinary share rate was 8.5 per cent, the composite income tax rate was 25.5 per cent. The cost of term shares to building societies, including taxation, was therefore 12.08, 12.75, 13.42, 14.09, and 14.76 per cent respectively for two, three, four, five and six year term shares. Losses were made on shares in excess of three year terms.

The BSA and the registrar have stressed the potential dangers of term shares. To quote the BSA: 'before contemplating the issue of such shares, careful consideration should be given to the long term implications and the effect on the society's operating margin and reserves.'[1]

A particular problem of term shares is the management of maturity dates. Again, to quote the BSA: 'consideration will have to be given to the pattern of maturity dates, the new terms that will have to be offered to retain the investments at maturity, or the provision of sufficient liquid funds to cover possible withdrawals.'[2] Concerning open-ended term shares, the Chief Registrar of Friendly Societies even felt it necessary to issue some sober warnings:

> there is clearly no immediate cause for concern on this score — I emphasise that — but the trend induced by this kind of issue [term shares] leaves me with a feeling of slight unease for the future. It may be that any real problem arising from these shares is more likely to come after the expiry of the qualification period, as up to the end of five years societies are paying only premium rates for term money.
>
> It hardly needs pointing out that, other things being equal, the task of servicing payment of a fixed addition of 2% on a variable interest rate become comparatively greater as interest rates fall.
>
> We are all aware of the recent pressure on margins. There are few indications that this pressure will be much eased in the period ahead. For some societies at least it may well increase.
>
> Any assumption that the demand for mortgage funds will remain high enough and interest-sensitive enough over the next five years or so to enable societies to pass on the higher costs to borrowers seems to me also to be taking a bit of a gamble. In saying this, I not only have in mind inherent uncertainties about the level of demand for mortgage funds over the next few years. I am also thinking of the possibility of a further increase in competition from the banks and other institutions.[3]

The amount of term share business, then, is critical to the profitability of a society, especially so as the movement tends towards the longer term shares. The effect of these developments on society profitability is illustrated in table 16: 1972 was the last year in which mortgage interest exceeded interest on shares and

Table 16 Building society aggregate performance (£ million)

	1970	1972	1974	1976	1978	1980	1982
Mortgage interest	702	945	1689	2288	2770	5912	7032
Shares and deposit interest	(692)	(928)	(1766)	(2397)	(2911)	(6223)	(7465)
Margin	10	17	(77)	(109)	(141)	(311)	(433)
Investment income	97	132	294	530	661	1072	1466
Other income	24	33	31	55	75	116	170
Management expenses	(68)	(103)	(145)	(237)	(363)	(579)	(869)
Corporation tax	(26)	(31)	(40)	(95)	(90)	(112)	(117)
Surplus	37	48	63	144	142	186	217
Asset disposal profits	15	28	11	43	70	62	308
Additions to reserves	52	76	74	187	212	248	525

Note: Brackets indicate negative numbers.
Source: Annual Reports of the Chief Registrar of Friendly Societies

deposits. It was also the year when term shares were first introduced. Nowadays, society profits are dependent on commissions earned and investment income — although, in fact, the proportion of funds in investments has changed little.

The level of management expenses at which a society is operating, for its size (the management expense ratio, the ratio between yearly management costs and total assets) and the proportion of its funds raised in term shares are the critical variables for society profitability. Figure 3 shows the relationship in the 1980 aggregate figures for the entire movement.

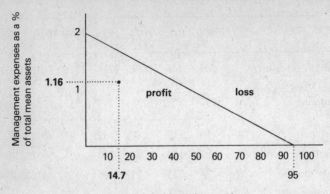

.... movement average

Example a society with 50% of total funds in term shares would have to keep management expenses below 1% of total mean assets to remain profitable

Figure 3 Break-even line between management and expense ratio and term shares, 1980 data.
Note: The BSA stopped publishing term share data after 1980, so it is not possible to calculate the critical percentages for subsequent years.
Source: Accountancy, October 1981.

Operating losses and investment gains

The inevitable question is: As profits are not guaranteed, but are earned only by prudent and economical management, and are going to become more difficult to earn in the future if competition on both fronts is to continue, how are societies making up their profits, and are they all doing so satisfactorily?

Table 16 shows how important the class 'other income less expenditure' has become. It largely represents capital profits on the sale of investments, mainly gilt-edged government securities ('gilts'). Some societies are heavily dependent upon successful gilts trading for their profits. It was revealed in *The Sunday Times* on 15

January 1984, that there were as many as 20 societies heavily dependent upon gilts trading. The main reason was, that if successful, they could earn a higher return than on mortgages, and without the hassle of checking title deeds and managing impoverished mortgagors, etc.

Until recently profits from gilts could be obtained by building societies virtually tax-free. First, by holding gilts for more than one year, capital gains were tax free. Second, by selling *cum div* just before the dividend payment they could obtain their accumulated interest as capital gains.

Some building societies actively traded in gilts and avoided taxation. They would buy low-coupon bonds which were designed to provide returns as capital gains. These would be held for a year and a day and sold *cum div*. Some societies with operating tax losses to spare could afford to take some gilts profits inside a year — if it was worth it.

But the dependence upon gilts has posed problems. First, there was the over-riding fear that societies could be identified by the tax authorities as gilts traders — which of course some were — and tax them as such: at 40 per cent on their interest received and capital gains alike. This in fact happened in February 1984. Second, undue dependence on gilts trading raised a building society's operating risk significantly. High returns on gilts were not assured. Large capital losses could be made. Societies would be prevented from selling a gilt until a profit was made. Profitability could be squeezed. To quote Tony Levene:

> Even the most inexpert manager could make a tolerable job of a low coupon portfolio. The volatile jungle of high coupon stocks — exactly the area where the New Cross Building Society came unstuck — is another matter.[4]

Finally, dependence upon gilts profits provided considerable accounting problems and embarrassment for the movement.

The presentation of building society accounts is governed by Section 78, Building Societies Act 1962, and in recent years by the Building Societies' (Accounts and Annual Return) Regulations 1976 (as amended in 1980). Schedule 1 to the regulations sets out the form in which the revenue and appropriation account should be presented. Here are listed the main forms of income (interest on mortgages, interest on investments and bank deposits and 'other income'), and expenditure. Corporation tax is then deducted. Exceptional items are then added and subtracted, and the net surplus transferred to reserves.

There is no specific reference to profits on the realization of investments, other than a requirement under Regulation 4 (a) for material amounts, less the corporation tax relating thereto, to be separately disclosed. Schedule 2 of the regulations sets out the form of the annual return in which Part 2, Section A, is an analysis of income. Here 'normal income' is distinguished from 'exceptional or non-recurrent income', and profits on the realization of investments are not listed as normal income.

It may be taken then that they are exceptional, or non-recurrent income. Therefore, although this is not explicitly stated, it is implicit from elsewhere in the regulations that profits on the realization of investments were not to be treated as 'normal income' (in the same way, losses are not to be treated as 'normal expenditure') and were therefore 'below the line' items. Traditionally they have been treated in this way; a view which the BSA had traditionally backed. To quote their guidebook:

Extraordinary items and prior year adjustments (SSAP6)

3.58 One of the effects of this standard on building societies is that profits and losses on sales of investments would need to be included in the surplus for the year, i.e., 'above the line', as such items are regarded as part of the ordinary activities of a building society. Adjustments relating to prior year taxation provisions would also need to be shown above the line before arriving at the surplus for the year.

3.59 Traditionally however building societies have included profits or losses on the sales of investments 'below the line' since to include them 'above the line' could cause serious distortions in the operating results for a year. The prescribed form of Revenue and Appropriation Account however permits these apparently conflicting practices to be reconciled by enabling such items to be shown below the first balance struck ('SURPLUS') but above the second balance

('NET SURPLUS TRANSFERRED TO GENERAL
RESERVE').[5]

Not all societies have accounted for profits on the realization of
investments in this way. I calculated that there were five medium-
sized societies that treated them 'above the line' in their 1981
accounts.[6] *If such investment profits had been recorded below the
line in three instances, they would have disclosed 'operating losses' as
conventionally defined (See Table 17).*
It should not be inferred that these societies were intentionally
concealing trading losses. Because of their gilts trading strategies,
in which societies took their investment returns largely as capital
gains rather than as interest payments, the 'interest on investment'
figure in the account became so understated (arguable artificially)
that some societies found it appropriate to include capital gains
'above the line', as they were 'capitalised interest' rather than true
capital items. In any case, it may be argued that societies could not
be accused of concealment, if an investor could reconstruct the
income and expenditure statement, although these gains were not
split between the accumulated interest portion and the speculative
gains portion.
A decision over whether the treatment of such items above or
below the line presented a true and fair view had to be made by the
auditors concerned. The auditors of three of the five societies
concerned are large nationwide firms who are very likely to audit
other societies. If the practice of hundreds of other societies and
the guidelines of the BSA indicated that profits and losses on the
sale of investments should have been recorded below the line, there
must have been a serious question for the auditors concerned,
whether treating these above the line presented a fair picture.
These comments relate only to the accounts up to and including
1982, and it is fair to add that this was a treatment accepted by the
Registry of Friendly Societies, who also legislated to this effect in
late 1983.
In the case of those societies who would have reported losses
had investment profits been recorded below the line, this had
previously been normal procedure. However in only one case was
there any mention of this change in accounting policy. It would

Table 17 Societies changing accounting treatment of investment gains

Society	1977	1978	1979	1980	1981	1982	Auditors
Birmingham & Bridgwater (from July 82)	OP BL	OP BL	OP AL	OP AL	OP AL	OP AL	Deloitte Haskins & Sells, Birmingham
Coventry Economic	OP BL	OL AL	OP AL	OL AL	OL AL	OP AL	Ernst & Whinney, London
Midshires	OP BL	OP BL	OL AL	OL AL	OP AL	OL AL	Deloitte Haskins & Sells, Birmingham
Town & Country	OP BL	OP BL	OL AL	OP AL	OP AL	OL AL	Thomas May & Co., Leicester
Gateway	OP BL	OP BL	OP BL	OP BL	OP AL	OP AL	Coopers & Lybrand London
Leicester	OP BL	OP BL	OP BL	OP BL	OP AL	OP AL	Thomson McLintock & Co., London
London & South of England*				OP AL	OP AL	OP** AL	Hale & Co., MacIntyre Hudson
Anglia	OP BL	OP BL	OP BL	OP BL	OP BL	OP AL	Coopers & Lybrand to 1981; Hale & Co., MacIntyre Hudson 1982

Continued / . . .

Table 17 Continued / . . .

Society	1977	1978	1979	1980	1981	1982	Auditors
Scarborough	OP BL	OP BL	OP BL	OP BL	OP BL	OP BL	Coulson & Co., Scarborough OL, AL. Year to 1 May 1983

* Formed by way of merger 1980, merged with Anglia, 1983
** OL to 4.4.83
Notes: BL–Below the line: this includes those societies using the compromise intermediate method of accounting suggested in the BSA guidebook, para 3.59 (see page 78); AL–Above the line; OP– Operating profit; OL–Operating loss.

appear therefore, that the decision to record these items below or above the line was not necessarily considered an accounting policy change in those other cases. The circumstances surrounding these changes are presented in Table 17.

This has posed the building societies concerned with a tricky problem. The building societies movement was strongly divided as to uniform accounting treatment. While many societies, including some of the very large ones, did not trade so actively in this way, there was little need for the conventional accounting treatment of gains to alter. The obvious solution was for those societies affected to split their investment gains into that part which was accrued interest and put it 'above the line'; and that part which came about from successful (or unsuccessful) buying and selling and put it 'below the line'. But there was reluctance. It put in question the continuance of the beneficial treatment of these profits as capital gains. The taxation authorities might see these gains as trading gains, (that would be the implication of the suggested accounting treatment) and tax them at 40 per cent. A second problem concerns how the 'real' capital gain, or loss, was calculated. Should it include a portion of the premium on the redemption of the security? If so, how much? Should all losses be brought in immediately, or should they be spread over the duration of the security? Were these figures of any meaning, given that the security would probably be sold before redemption? And so on.

In any case it would be inappropriate to be seen to 'change the rules to fit the game'. To quote the authoritative text on building society accounting:

> It is acknowledged that these entries may not be acceptable in their entirety to all building society practitioners and it is certainly not claimed that they represent the only correct method of investment accounting. Over a period of years, any of a number of different accounting methods will produce much the same result. What is important above all, however, is that a society should be *consistent* in its investment accounting methods from one year to another and that techniques should not be changed to suit the circumstances of particular transactions of particular periods.[7]

It would be reasonable to expect the accountancy bodies to have sorted out such technical matters. They did not do so; the policy of the Accounting Standards Committee was not to get involved in designing accounting standards for individual industries. The BSA set up a committee to look at these matters. A confidential report was issued in December 1983, making tentative proposals involving gains (arising from selling gilts *cum div*) and pure capital gains. At the time it was felt that not all member societies would agree any set proposals. However, with the tax changes the inclusion of trading gains above the line is now no longer such a sensitive matter and agreement on these 'rule changes' is more likely.

But the societies still had to prepare their accounts, and for 1983 there was no agreed treatment. The Registrar of Friendly Societies acknowledged this. Section 5 of the 1983 Building Societies (Accounts and Annual Return) Regulations recognized that societies might wish to place their investment gains above the line and that there might be an eventual BSA compromise. (These regulations came just in time, going through on 9 December 1983.)

Until such a time as these matters are resolved, published financial information may well be fundamentally misleading.

Consider the information published in the *Building Societies Gazette* (the industry's independent magazine) where a monthly feature is made of individual societies' financial results in a section entitled 'Progress Reports'. Among the statistics provided is operating surplus. This is defined as:

> the ratio which a society's operating surplus — i.e the surplus after corporation tax but before exceptional items 'below the line' — bears to the mean total assets. *Net Surplus* ratio is the ratio which the net surplus transferred from the revenue and appropriation account to the general reserve bears to the mean total assets.

The Birmingham & Bridgewater, Coventry Economic, Midshires, and Town & Country reported operating surpluses. No mention was made that these contained investment gains 'above the line' and (however justified) that if they had reported in a similar way to the other societies they would have shown deficits.

Second, if an investor wishes to compare the financial performance of societies they should treat investment gain in a similar way. If they cannot agree on this, at least sufficient data must be available to make the necessary transformation. This is an important matter (especially in the light of New Cross) when it is vital to know what portion of investment gains may be interpreted as non-recurrent, speculative profits. The 1983 regulations did not ensure this. They acted against it by making it more easy for societies to place gains above the line and with no analysis of their nature.

Profit inadequacies generally

It has been argued that the adoption of excessive policies of growth maximization (too much reliance upon long term shares) and expense preference (unnecessarily large branch networks) can lead to insufficient profits being generated. *Over a long period this could threaten societies' financial stability. This would be made worse if societies placed undue reliance upon high-risk gilts dealing to finance those policies.*

Such a situation could arise when there are either pressures on margins from high interest rates or excessive competition from outside the movement, or where both occur together. The late 1970s and early 1980s saw examples of this. In the early 1980s extreme competition came from both the government and the banks.

The competition for savings was led by the National Savings movement in an attempt to help balance the Chancellor of the Exchequer's books. The competition for the provision of housing finance has also been stepped up by the banks, notably Barclays, increasing the amount of money they are prepared to lend on property, and offering highly competitive mortgage rates. The net effect, as the government authorities saw it, was that the banks were merely replacing the home loan finance siphoned out of the building societies by National Savings.

The question must be asked: Did profit insufficiency exist on any large scale during this period and, if so, were the causes those suggested above? The period 1978–80 was tested using a large sample of active building societies. A measure of sufficiency of profit is available from the building society regulations which define the minimum amount of reserves that must be held by a society according to its size. Our criterion for a profit adequacy, therefore, is whether the profit earned in a year is large enough to match that required by the corresponding increase in assets.[8]

The following variables were investigated as explanations for any profit inadequacy.

(1) *Growth policies* as measured by the annual percentage increase in total assets. It is assumed that differences in growth rates between societies are indicative of managerial growth policies. Managerial policies on products offered, and the timing of them, largely account for variations in society growth rates.

(2) *Expense preference* policies as revealed in the management expense ratio (operating expenses/ total assets), a measure of unit operating costs.

(3) *The ability/inability to cover excesses in 1 and 2 with other income.* This could be done by means of (i) a higher rate on some mortgages, say, using a differential rate scheme (as indicated in the average rate on mortgages), (ii) making large capital gains on investments (as indicated in the extraordinary-items

figure in the annual accounts), and (iii) by attracting high commissions, etc.

A statistical technique called discriminant analysis was used to distinguish between the groups of societies making 'sufficient' and 'insufficient' profits.[9]

The results for 1978 and 1980 were quite similar.[9] The growth rate variable for 1978 was particularly significant, together with the extraordinary-items variable. This would indicate that a high growth rate threatened profitability, and the society's success in achieving satisfactory profitability was dependent upon gilts trading. The operating expenses ratio was significant but played a smaller part in discriminating between the two groups. The shares and deposits interest rate variable (an indication of the expense of terms offered to savers) made a small contribution to the discrimination. The mortgage interest rate and other income variables were not significant, which indicates they were not used to cover the effects on profitability and expense preference policies. This was largely true of the results for 1980. Again the three significant variables were growth rates, management expenses and extraordinary items. Management expenses was the most successful discriminator.

The results for 1979, when more building societies disclosed profits regarded as insufficient by our criteria, were rather different. Here again management expenses was the major discriminating variable. Extraordinary items had little significance. The remaining variables had roughly similar discriminating contributions. These included growth rates, the major discriminating variable in 1978, other income, mortgage interest rate and shares and deposits rates variables which for other years had little discriminatory significance.

We may conclude from this study that discretionary policies of expense preference and growth are responsible for some building societies earning, arguably, a perilously inadequate profit during difficult trading periods. However, the study failed to establish the overall importance of the one factor over the other (growth preference, expense preference) consistently throughout the three years examined. Of the ways in which societies may cover these additional costs — increased rates on mortgages (differential mortgages), other income (for example, commissions), and capital gains on investment dealings — the first two were found to be insignificant in distinguishing the two profitability groups. The inference is that they did not help to alleviate profit inadequacy to any significant degree. (Differential mortgages were later disbanded by most societies.) On the other hand, investment gains were found to be particularly important. Societies were therefore more dependent on them. But a failure to achieve these 'one-off' gains resulted in profit inadequacy of some societies. In terms of policy, undue dependence on such a source of income, which is unassured, is imprudent and potentially disastrous. For such gains to subsidize managerial policies of expense preference and growth preference is irresponsible.

The closure of the New Cross Building Society

In January 1984 the New Cross proved to be just such a society. It failed because it went for growth unwisely by offering particularly high premia on interest to investors. It attempted to finance these by differential rates on large mortgages and, of course, by dealing in gilts.

To some extent the New Cross downfall was a symptom of general economic conditions. In 1983 interest rates were relatively low; premia on term shares and other high interest accounts made profits more difficult to achieve. A promised premium of 2 per cent may have been manageable when interest rates were around 15 per cent but when they fall to 7 or 8 per cent and these premiums still have to be paid, things become more difficult. 1983 was also a particularly difficult year in which to make speculative capital gains on gilts. Interest rates (which largely determine the prices of · gilts) were relatively stable and movements were unpredictable.

The rise of the New Cross reflected the ambition of its main driving force, its chair, Reg Rowland. The assets of New Cross soared from only £6 million when Rowland took over the sleepy society in 1975 to nearly £120 million in 1983. Rowland's background was not building societies; he was a chartered accountant and involved in property speculation. In the 1960s his main interest was rubber plantation companies and property development.

But the New Cross was not so untypical of the movement. Although its growth rate worried certain parts of the building societies movement and the Registry, other societies experienced high growth.

The New Cross attracted concern from the Registry of Friendly Societies for breaking certain statutory regulations. It exceeded the 10 per cent limit for special advances by a small margin. When for example in 1980, the Peckham Mutual made special advances of almost double the permitted level it was let off with a warning. The New Cross also failed to meet its minimum reserve ratio in both 1979 and 1981, but the Registry of Friendly Societies removed its threat of closure, after receiving assurances about its future. Other societies fell below this limit from time to time during the 1970s.

The New Cross case raises many questions. Are the statutory financial criteria satisfactory? Are the policing arrangements by the Registry satisfactory? It would seem that the answer to both of these is 'no'. Effective control must attend to causes rather than effects. Should the New Cross have been allowed to be managed so aggressively? Should there be regulation addressed specifically to high growth societies? What are the penalties and consequences of breaking the statutory reserve, liquidity and special advances ratios?

Finally, should societies be allowed to rely upon gilts in this way?

Until these questions are satisfactorily answered by extant legislation it is reasonable to expect more cases such as the New Cross.

Final remarks

The consequences of the combination of high cost funding and excessive branching were recognized by the majority within the building society industry before the collapse of the New Cross. The chief registrar has spoken out on the dangers of term shares. They have been dismissed as 'old fashioned' by the industry. Nevertheless, they continue to increase as a percentage of total funding.

It has been shown here that such policies are paid for by dealing in the government securities market. This is not without risk and we identified some societies with excessive branching and term share policies that earned 'inadequate' profits because of insufficient investment profits. A major reason for the downfall of the New Cross was its undue and unsuccessful reliance upon high-risk gilts trading. The importance of investment profits has caused considerable embarrassment to the building societies movement. Firstly, because they have been spotted for dealing in gilts — or at least some societies have — and as a result they have all lost their considerable tax benefits.[10] Secondly, they have been seen to be in considerable disarray concerning the accounting treatment of investment gains — mainly because of their reluctance to threat them as trading income.

But is this undue reliance upon gilts trading to be accepted? The purpose of building societies is to provide mortgage finance. By holding excess funds in investments and gilts in order to pursue excessive expansionist policies they were acting quite outside their role as building societies. To this extent the decision to tax gilts dealing is to be applauded, if it has the effect that societies will become more willing to offer mortgages. Of course it is hoped that any additional tax collected by the Inland Revenue will go back to housing in some way; say by increasing the mortgage tax relief.

One question remains: how will those societies previously so dependent on gilts trading be affected? We are unlikely to know until their 1984 accounts are published. No doubt any losses will be treated below the line!

8. 'Managerial diversion'

The American experience

The development of the American mutual savings and loan association (SLA) provides an important insight into the operations of the UK building societies. The SLAs are direct descendants of the UK building society. The orginal SLAs were small local co-operatives, organized solely to handle savings and make real estate loans. All members were both savers and borrowers and the associations were dissolved when each member had received and repaid his loan, as in the original building societies. Until 1950 the typical SLA was small, mutual and local. The Federal Home Loan Bank Board recognized this, concluded that SLAs were too small to afford competent full-time managers, and acted to attract them by allowing existing SLAs to seek related business outside, such as insurance which could be combined with real estate financing, mortgage brokerage, title insurance and so on. If was felt that the SLA would prosper under a management both involved and experienced in these aspects of real estate. There were no obvious 'conflicts of interest'. In fact, the arrangement was considered a distinct advantage.

Tech, expert on the development of the SLAs, writes:

> As the savings and loan industry evolved, it became
> increasingly common for directors not only to receive
> compensation for services performed as officers and lawyers
> of their respective organization — as did mutual savings bank
> trustees — but also to profit from positions of financial
> interests with other organizations to which business was
> directed from their savings and loan association.[1]

Nichols, authority on the operations of SLAs, develops the implications:

> A distinguishing characteristic of the mutual is the apparent omnipotence of management, which rarely accounts for its actions and policies as it must in the conventional stock corporation. Though the saver provides the funds which the association lends, he owns only his savings. Referred to as a member, he typically surrenders his proxy to management upon the opening of the account. Because there are no association owners to whom profits or net earnings are distributed . . . The managers of mutual establishments can be likened to 'self-perpetuating autocracies' . . . The problem facing management in the mutual is the conversion of its power into personal gain of some form. That management can do this is clear and obvious since there is no internal check or power capable of frustrating it. Under the restraint that the management cannot take out profits or sell control, the ordinary and most apparent avenues open to management are (1) to share in the success of the firm through salary increases; (2) to take a larger share of the establishment's income in the form of amenities; and (3) to divert income to other proprietary firms owned by the managers. In the first two instances, expenses are increased with obvious effects on both the output of the firm and the accumulation of new capital. The ability to increase expenses must depend upon an absence of competitive cost-cutting and price competition . . . It is not to mutual management's interest to permit price to ration. Frustrated borrowers are compelled to make competitive offers not for the services of the savings and loan association but for the service of the management-owned affiliate. By this means, monopoly profit is diverted to management.[2]

The point is that the conversion of management's power into personal gain of some form is not only inevitable but is associated with deliberate creation of disequilibrium or shortage situations.

Nichol's notion of 'managerial diversion' extends the concept of managerial discretion by stating that not only are managers motivated to maximize their direct income (in salaries and so on) and indirect income (status, for instance), but also to channel further income to themselves by various covert means. The only difference between managerial behaviour in 'mutual' organizations and profit making organizations is that there are major restrictions upon the amount of direct income that is acceptable, and that managers have to look for methods of diverting it.

Nichols presents all types of evidence, including the discovery of widespread nepotism and interconnecting businesses surrounding the SLAs in order to show how SLA managers share in profits. Nichols is enormously cynical of the practice of mutuality. He concludes:

> If mutuality is characterized by public benevolence and stock ownership by private cupidity, it might be preferable for the nation to opt for the latter. Mutuality is a euphemism to shield powerful restrictive forces from the public scrutiny.[3]

Meanwhile in the UK . . .

The 2nd November 1954 marked the beginning of a property boom in the UK that was to last almost 20 years. That afternoon Nigel Brich, Minister of Works in the Conservative government, announced to the House of Commons that building licences were to be dropped: 'Licences are now issued freely in nearly all areas and neither the cost nor the inconvenience caused to architects and contractors can any longer be justified.' There were cheers from the Conservative benches. Building societies became big business. For the first time they started setting up many branches, and there was huge expansion due to the encouragement the government was also giving them in tax advantages to stimulate the building of new housing.

An aspect of this noticed by the eminent building societies historian, Cleary,[4] was the rise of a new type of building society. As the law stood there was nothing illegal in it: a group of people form both a limited company and a building society. The limited company raises sufficient funds, perhaps by way of a very short-term loan as bridging finance, to purchase a property, and immediately repays the loan from the money obtained by mortgaging the property to the companion building society. As long as the building society takes care to ensure that the property is reasonable security for the loan, and does not invest too much of its funds in loans to these companies and especially to any single company, such activities would be considered more or less acceptable building society practices. If such considerations are not borne in mind by the building society, then there are dangers of course.

A type of transaction popular at this time grew out of the prevailing rent control regulations and the disparity between the vacant possession value of a house and its value with a sitting tenant. Here were opportunities for profit which some people exploited with the help of building society funds. People in control of a society could form a limited company to buy a block of rent-controlled property at a low price, based on the low net return of such property. Because of its access to the funds of its companion building society, the company could then sell these houses to the sitting tenants at prices well above those paid by the company. The building society offered the sitting tenant generous mortgage terms with high advances, even over 100 per cent of the purchase price, and long periods of repayments; at the same time the society might not look too closely at the borrower's ability to repay the loan.

The profitability of such operations, although their true nature was concealed from their investors, made it possible for these building societies to offer higher interest rates than societies conducting more normal activities.

There were more sophisticated and dangerous techniques of using building society funds for speculative purposes, such as taking over companies rather than modest blocks of rent-controlled property.

The technique was adaptable to other uses. Hotels, farms and industrial properties might be purchased at prices that included a considerable element of goodwill; and provided the building society was sufficiently liberal in its valuation (a not unlikely eventuality if the valuer was a director of both the company and the society) the society could legally advance the whole of the purchase price, or indeed more. Investors in such building societies, believing that their money was secured by mortgages on mainly owner-occupied property, were a good deal more vulnerable than they imagined.

Those sections of the prevailing law, the 1894 Act, which sought to reveal such transactions by requiring details of all advances in excess of £5,000, were frustrated by making a series of small advances, each backed by a separate mortgage deed. The most difficult problem the law presented was the need for bridging finance, since assets had to be the property of the company before the building society could make any loan. But in some cases this problem was simply overcome by sending cheques for advances before the property had been purchased; the society in effect provided the bridging finance.

The registrar made strenuous investigations to curb the activities of these 'rogue' societies. There were 33 such investigations between 1953 and 1959 alone. He also made orders forbidding them to advertise for funds and publicized the dangers they presented to the investing public. In his report for 1954, he wrote: 'a disturbing feature . . . in recent years has been the tendency on the part of certain societies to advance substantial sums of money to companies or groups of companies.[5] Consequently in 1956 he altered his requirement regarding the information to be given in the annual return societies made to him; particulars had now to be given 'of mortgages where, in respect of any one borrower, there was more than one mortgage and the total indebtedness at the end of the society's financial year exceeded £25,000'.[6]

The resulting figures showed that substantial loans were made by many societies. While they did not play a significant part in the operations of most ordinary societies, there were a number of cases, including three of the 20 largest societies, where they exceeded $7\frac{1}{2}$ per cent of total assets. Rogue societies responded to this attempt to force them to disclose their large loans by creating chains of subsidiary companies, making only one advance to each. In 1956 one society made 26 simultaneous advances to a series of companies, each of £9,860.

In 1959 the registrar acted again, by extending the definition of the phrase 'one borrower' to include:

companies or subsidiary companies under common control and borrowers acting as nominees for one nominator — an indication is also required in respect of such mortgages where any director of the society or nominee of a director is a borrower or is a partner or shareholder of a borrower.'[7]

By this time it was clear that the registrar needed greater powers if he was to act effectively in curbing these excesses. In February 1959 it was revealed that the government was considering fresh legislation. However, it took the revelations concerning the State Building Society, later in the year, to add a sense of urgency.

The government's Bill was introduced in March 1960 and became the 1960 Building Societies Act. The activities of the rogue societies were controlled by the first two sections of the Act. 'Special advances' were not to exceed 10 per cent of the total advances made by a society in any one year. A 'special advance' was defined as any advance of over £5,000, or an additional advance which raised a mortgagor's total debt over £5,000, or any advance to a body corporate. Where more than 10 per pent of a society's funds were already advanced in these ways, the Act limited its ability to make special advances still more closely, so that eventually no society would have more than 10 per cent of its assets so applied.

The 1960 Act was consolidated into the 1962 Act. The provision regarding special advances did not change although the £5,000 definition would periodically be revised.

The State Building Society scandal

The State Building Society was incorporated in 1931 and for many years was a very small society. Because of the sort of lending just discussed, its assets grew rapidly during the 1950s. In 1952 they amounted to £0.5 million, in 1958 they were £10.5 million and by 1959 they were £15 million. The chairman of the State was a 78-year-old retired chartered accountant, Mr. Noel Cow. The remainder of the board consisted of an estate agent, a local government official, a retired bookmaker and the son-in-law to the chairman. Mr Murray, 68, a surveyor and a registered architect, was the managing director *and* secretary. The society's official solicitors were Harewood & Co., which consisted of two partners, Mr Grunwald and Mr Kauter.

The Jasper Group of property companies started in 1956 with an association between H.O. Jasper, Mr Grunwald, and the directors of the State Building Society.

Their first property dealings were through a company called Stevenson (Westminster) Ltd, which owned property and was financed by mortgages from the State. In 1956 these amounted to £260,000. The company bought property in bulk and sold it in individual units to tenants. Both sides of the transactions were financed by mortgage advances from the State. This was the usual pattern for the later Jasper companies.

It was known that the Chief Registrar of Friendly Societies disliked the close connection between the State and Stevenson (Westminster) Ltd, and Mr Cow and Mr Murray decided to transfer the properties and mortgages to one or more public companies. To this end Cotton Plantations (COP) and Capital & Provincial were acquired by Mr Grunwald. At the time COP was a 'shell' company, and Capital & Provincial owned and operated a chain of cinemas. In order to avoid the disapproval of the Registrar of Friendly Societies, Murray did not join the boards of these companies. The remaining Stevenson (Westminster) properties were transferred to other newly formed companies owned by Mr Cow and Mr Murray, which received advances from the society secured on these properties. The previous mortgage advances of similar amounts were repaid. In the same month, these companies were sold to Capital & Provincial, which found the purchase price out of advances made by the society on the security of its cinemas.

At about the same time the control of a third property company called National Model Dwellings (NMD) was acquired with the assistance of advances from the society which were ultimately secured on that company's properties. NMD then purchased shares in four property companies owned by Mr Murray.

As a result of the sale of their property interests to these three companies of the Jasper Group, Mr Cow and Mr Murray became large shareholders. They gave some of their shares to Mrs Clarke, assistant secretary of the State Building Society. All their shares were placed in a 'pool' on the understanding that they would not be sold for at least one year. Mr Murray was by far the largest member. The shares were held by bank nominees and operated by Mr Grunwald. Between 1957 and 1959 the Jasper Group expanded by further takeovers. The pool played an important part in some of these transactions by receiving shares in newly acquired companies in exchange for shares of earlier Jasper companies already held. The effect of these exchanges was that, by September, 1959, the majority of the share capital of both COP and Capital & Provincial was held by other companies of the Jasper Group. Mr Grunwald was managing director of most of the Jasper companies and these inter-company transactions were usually carried out through Harewood & Co. clients' account, the inter-company holdings being registered in the name of bank nominees to order of Harewood & Co. In the later takeovers other clients of Harewood & Co. appear to have participated, and in some cases there was no evidence that the original pool was concerned. Through the introduction of these new clients of Harewood & Co. and the substantial purchases of shares by other companies in the Jasper Group, the basis of control was widened and altered.

Most of the cash required for the purchase of shares taken over in the name of H. Jasper and Co. Ltd was provided by the companies themselves, either through cash balances held by those companies or by means of cash borrowed from the State on mortgages of property owned by their subsidiaries. When agreement had been reached with the directors of the company to be taken over, and an offer made to the remaining shareholders and accepted by them, Grunwald and Jasper became directors; and before the date for completing the purchase of the shares they were in a position to arrange for the company to buy assets consisting of properties belonging to Mr Murray or, after the takeover of Capital & Provincial News Theatres Ltd when there were no such properties left, shares in Mr Murray, Mr Grunwald and Mrs Clarke's pool. Payment for these assets then provided the necessary cash to complete the purchase of the shares.[8]

Before a bid was made for control of a property company, Mr Murray would inspect the properties concerned and assess the amount that the society would be prepared to advance on a mortgage. 'Bridging finance' was then obtained, partly from banks and partly from clients of Harewood & Co. Frequently, however, part of the 'bridging finance' was provided by the State which, having agreed to grant mortgage advances, sent the money to Harewood & Co. before the date at which purchase of control of the company was to be completed, and therefore, before the date at which Harewood & Co. were in a position to arrange for the corresponding mortgages.[9]

After control had been assured, legal charges on the properties of the newly acquired company were given to the State in respect of the money advanced by it and used as 'bridging finance'. In some cases the cash resources of the newly acquired company were used towards repaying 'bridging finance' provided by banks and other clients of Harewood & Co.

At 30 September 1959, the State had outstanding £7.7 million from the Jasper group. Of this £3.3 million consisted of amounts sent to Harewood & Co. for advances mainly to a company called Lintang which did not receive the money and for which the State had no security.

Major partners in many of the takeovers were property men Gerson Berger and his son, Sigismund. They may well not have known of the State Building Society and the way in which Grunwald and Murray were operating. Sigismund Berger first met Grunwald in 1954. At the beginning of 1959 they obtained a 'shell' company, renamed Reliable Property Ltd., to hold a number of properties previously belonging to the Bergers. S. and G. Berger became directors, Jasper was the chair, and Grunwald the managing director. The Bergers were the majority shareholders.

The Lintang affair has been described as 'the biggest post-war financial scandal'. Lintang had been floated in March 1959 in one of the most exciting scenes every witnessed on the Stock Exchange, stimulated by the dual magic of a new property issue and the name of Maxwell Joseph. Marriot writes:

The commotion caused by the arrival of Lintang was said to be even greater than the sensational rush for Morris Motors nearly thirty years before. When the house [of the Stock

Exchange] opened at 9 o'clock, half an hour earlier than usual to cope with the rush, the queue of 400 brokers eager to buy Lintang, some waiting from the early hours, stretched most of the length of Throgmorton Street. The shares had been offered at 11s. 6d. each. They started off at 16s. and within minutes shot up to 22s. In effect investors at large were deciding that a company, valued by experts in the offer at £3.6 million, was immediately worth £7 million. This hullabaloo over Lintang had all the ingredients of a shanty town gold rush. It is fantastic in retrospect that a share with net assets, recently valued, of 10s. apiece should have been lapped up at once at over double that. But this ignores the heady glamour of property shares bubbling up in 1959, and the unquestioning faith in the heroes of the property world.[10]

In July 1959 Grunwald approached Maxwell Joseph with a view to taking over Lintang. It would cost £6 or £7 million. Jasper was to put up £1 million, the Bergers £1 million, £1 million was to come from Martin's Bank, half secured on shares in Reliable Properties, and half secured on shares in the 'pool'. Most of the remainder was to be put up by Mr Murray. In the event, not all the money was raised, Jasper did not provide all his and the Bergers only provided £0.5 million. Mr Murray provided £3,255,500, in the form of mortgage loans by the State to subsidiaries of Lintang. Accordingly 32 cheques were sent to Harewood & Co.

According to Board of Trade Inspectors[11] there were no letters of application for the mortgages by the companies concerned and many of them were not even formed when the mortgage monies were granted. It was also discovered that the minutes of the State concerning the mortgages were falsified.

The 51 per cent stake in Lintang held by Maxwell Joseph was paid off and Jasper and Grunwald were appointed to the board. It was the failure to raise sufficient funds and purchase the remaining share capital which brought about the crisis that September.

The uncompleted takeover caused the State to have an unsecured debt owing by Harewood & Co. for £3,255,500. Murray and Grunwald were charged with fraudulent conversion of the money and were eventually each sentenced to five years gaol.

As noted earlier in this chapter, the legal requirements at that time were the disclosure in a building society's annual return to the chief registrar of all mortgages granted exceeding £5,000. Particulars of any one borrower with total debt exceeding £25,000 were also required. By using subsidiary companies borrowing less than £25,000 and mortgages for less than £5,000 in each case, the reality of the position was completely obscured both from the chief registrar and from depositors. This occurred with the Lintang takeover and other large acquisitions.

The Berger family

Whilst some of the Jasper companies were mopped up by Maxwell Joseph in order to clear up the State deficit, others continued as part of the Berger empire.

Gerson Berger started in property in a small way. He would obtain a mortgage on a property and in a later period of rising prices would secure a second mortgage on the same property. This money would be used to buy new property and so his empire grew. It expanded rapidly during the 1950s and by the time of the State scandal Gerson Berger was said to be one of the richest men in London and possibly its largest landlord.

The Berger empire comprises around 400 interlocking companies. The registered office of many of them is 13-17 New Burlington Place, Regent Street, the address of their auditors, Cohen, Arnold & Co. Two of the largest today are public companies, Reliable Properties and Palmerston Investment Trust. These were first acquired by partnership with the Jasper group.

Despite having given substantial funds to charities, Gerson Berger was a multi-millionaire by 1960. When the property boom ended in 1973 many property companies simply went bankrupt. Berger's survived. Berger companies don't behave like usual landlords. They are property asset strippers. They buy rented property, wait for tenants to leave, and then redevelop it and sell it off, often on a long lease. A property with a sitting tenant is worth about 40 per cent of its value with vacant possession. Terry Dean, who runs the Berger Action Group told me:

The landlords allow properties to deteriorate to conditions of serious disrepair. If tenants living in bad conditions find it affects their health, they are inclined to look for somewhere better to live. That suits the landlord because he can redevelop the property and sell it at a huge profit on a long lease.

Ironically, Berger companies were about the last companies to continue letting out flats. However, since 1976, Berger companies have sought to sell anything they can — whole blocks or individual empty flats. This has resulted in most Berger blocks now having a mixture of tenants and owner-occupiers (technically called 'long leaseholders' who usually have bought a 99-year lease). This situation has helped Berger, because it has sometimes meant a less than united front from residents who perceive their interests differently. Bergers normally retain the freehold, and with it the power to appoint managing agents who supposedly maintain the property. So, far from being free of the Bergers, the purchasers are often even more firmly in their clutches.[12]

In 1977 Gerson Berger died at the age of 84. His son, Sigismund, took over his father's empire. Relatives of the Berger family include Hasias Lanfer, Rifka Gross and Milton Gross.

Aggrieved tenants from all walks of life have joined together to form BAG — the Berger Action Group. Its aim is to co-ordinate a campaign to put pressure on the government to take action against the Berger empire. Their first act was to hold a demonstration. They have been given £1,000 by Westminster City Council to fight the Bergers. The council has already struck one blow by no longer giving to speculative developers investment grants used to convert empty premises into modern flats. The council is serving public health notices and repair notices under the Building Acts on Berger property. It is also pressing the Department of Trade and Industry to take action against those many Berger companies whose accounts and returns are out of date at Companies Registration office.

Berger companies and the Britannia Building Society

Building society finance has been a major source of funds for the

Berger empire. The Britannia has lent many millions of pounds to these companies over the years. In just one year, 1981, the Britannia lent four Berger/Gross companies £1,139,000 (out of a total £1,430,800 special advances to all companies that year) and this was when the Berger empire was moving out of rented residential property.

A lot of this money was advanced on properties already owned by those companies, a practice which while not illegal is surely socially unacceptable for reasons discussed elsewhere. The loan of £25,000 to Bar Ltd was secured on Warnington Court, Croydon, already owned by that company. Of the £575,000 loan to Idens Estates Ltd, £190,000 was secured on the freehold of Purley Court, London, already owned by that company. The £260,000 advance to Zambra Investments (a Gross company) was secured on Lancaster Lodge, Kensington, and Princes Gate, Kingsway Worthing, already owned by that company. The accounts for the year to 31 March 1982 show that this money enabled Zambra to increase its 'loan debtors' from £322,000 to £539,000.

In 1982 the Britannia lent another £1,000,000. An advance of £150,000 was made to Parlmerston Investment Trust plc on a mortgage dated 17 March 1982: the accounts for Palmerston show that no properties were purchased during the year to 31 March 1982. Triplank Ltd received a loan of £265,000 accrued on property it already owned. Cabtell received £500,000 secured on property already owned. Cabtell originally obtained a mortgage on this property on 29 September 1959 from the State, when the company was set up as part of the Jasper/Berger partnership. This property (6 Hall Road, St John's Wood) was later remortgaged in 1964 with the Co-operative Building Society (later the Nationwide) and again in 1971 with the Nationwide. Finally, Nalper Properties received an advance of £145,000 on properties already owned. All these Britannia loans were made on 17 March, 1982.

The Lion and the Britannia Building Societies

From my researches of public records I have discovered a society which was being run largely to finance property development companies and which escaped public condemnation. This is the

Lion Building Society whose head office was at Hollington Court, Chislehurst, Kent, with branches in London and Reading.

At the end of 1959 the Lion had lent £4.3 million to just seven groups of borrowers out of its total of funds of £5.3 million. These included loans to property companies owned by some of the directors of the Lion (see figure 4). In addition, a large part of this was to a group of companies owned by Bernard Clarke and his wife. Bernard Clarke's brother was Dudley Clarke, official solicitor to the Lion. Bernard Clarke and his partners set up many small companies with minimal share capital (often £2), the remaining finance coming from the Lion. The auditor of the Lion was Toby Hoffman, a partner in Gerald Edelman & Co., 25 Harley Street. Hoffman had many outside interests and at one stage, through his company, Harley Street Securities Ltd, held shares in one of the Bernard Clarke companies. Gerald Edelman & Co. became auditors for the Clarke companies in 1976 and continue so today.

Such activities were not illegal. However, the huge proportion of the Lion's funds with these seven groups of borrowers made it impossible for the society to comply with the 1960 legislation concerning special advances. Nevertheless, my researches indicate that subsequent advances from the Lion to Clarke companies during 1960 approached £500,000. There were further loans in 1961 and 1962. The new legislation also required that from 1960 onwards special advances made during the year be listed in the society's annual return. These special advances to Clarke companies (the 1960 act made all advances to limited companies 'special') were not listed in the Lion's annual return. The Lion simply put a line through the relevant columns and entered no figures.

The Chief Registrar of Friendly Societies was aware of what was happening. It is on public record that he ordered two inspections of the Lion's books, one in 1958, the other in 1962. The subject of the investigation and the findings are now known. The situation was resolved however in 1964 when the Leek & Moorlands Building Society took over the Lion. (The Leek & Moorlands later became the Leek & Westbourne & Eastern Counties, through a merger in 1974, and in the same year changed its name to the Britannia.)

The Lion had five directors including S.R. Grandfield, general manager, and C.W.B. Purchas, secretary. Both of these, and most of the other staff, stayed on with the Leek and Moorlands; the other three directors retired. The head office and branches were not closed down and remain Britannia branch offices. In fact Hollington Court, Chislehurst, was the office for the Britannia for many years, with Mr Grandfield regional manager and Mr Purchas branch manager.

Bernard Clarke and Partners also still operate, albeit very privately. They operate from a mansion set in a huge estate, 'Southlands', just outside Tandridge, a small village in south Surrey. Access is by way of a mile-long private road. There are no business notices other than a simple sign, 'Enquiries'.

They are property speculators. They buy, sell and rent property throughout the country. Much of this involves large blocks of rented properties. These are sold off as and when the tenants leave. Like the Bergers, their profit is made on the price of the property with vacant possession. Bernard Clarke and Partners do not usually deal with the general public. They operate through local agents.

Prior to the Lion takeover, mortgage finance was obtained almost exclusively from the Lion. It continued with the Leek & Westbourne and, after it changed its name, the Britannia. In 1972, at the height of the property boom, they obtained £720,000 from the Leek & Westbourne. In that same year they obtained further advances: £290,000 from the Nationwide, and £325,000 from the Leicester.

What is remarkable about the Britannia loans is that although they were not illegal they were not for the promotion of home ownership but were for the purchase of property already owned by the Bernard Clarke family or another company in the group. Moreover, one of the properties mortgaged was *part of Hollington Court* itself, previously owned by Bernard and Dorothy Clarke!

In recent years Clarke companies have regularly obtained building society mortgage finance. These are as shown in Table 18.

Some of these were also refinancing transactions. The £50,000 to Citybrae from the Alliance was for the purchase of a property from Somarke Ltd, another Clarke company. The loan of £124,250 to Villagate was for properties, some of which were also already owned by other Clarke companies.

Table 18   Clarke companies obtaining building society mortgages

Company	Year	Building society mortgage (£)	
Jovine Ltd	1981	Britannia,	80,000
	1981	Alliance,	118,000
Citybrae Ltd	1980	Alliance,	50,000
	1982	Britannia,	54,000
Villagate Ltd	1981	Alliance,	124,250
	1982	Anglia,	225,000
		Bristol & West,	532,000
		Chatham Reliance,	250,000
		Britannia,	275,000
	1983	Nationwide,	250,000

The 1982 loan to Citybrae Ltd of £54,000 was omitted from the Britannia's annual return audited by Price Waterhouse. An amended return was submitted to the Registry of Friendly Societies in October 1983, nine months after the original. At the same time the Britannia also amended its annual returns for the years 1975, 1976, 1978 and 1979 concerning special advances including those to Berger companies. A further amended return for 1982 was submitted early in 1984.

There have been other discrepancies: a special advance to Villagate but later transferred to Jovine in 1981 had still not been registered with Companies Registration Office at the end of 1983 as required by company law.[13] The Registry has been investigating (not yet completed at the end of 1983), the issues arising from the apparent inaccuracies in the accounts of the Clarke companies. Ligmall (Sennan), Jovine, Citybrae and Villagate.[14] Since an article in *The Sunday Times* in February 1983,[15] there have been many Parliamentary questions by Ken Weetch MP, but by the end of 1983 the Chief Registrar of Friendly Societies has still made no comment and the significance (or otherwise) of these irregularities remained unknown.

The Alliance

Another group of property companies extensively financed by building society mortgages and almost exclusively from the Alliance involved the Coleman-Cohen family. Notable members of the family were the late Lord Lewis Cohen of Brighton, between 1945 and 1965 the managing director of the Alliance, and R.H. Coleman-Cohen, his brother and a partner in a large Brighton firm of estate agents, who was secretary of the society during the same period.

Maurice Cohen, another brother, was director, or usually managing director, of the property companies. In 1956 he was a director of 47 of them. I sampled 14 of these companies. With the exception of just one, which was a building company, they were property companies, almost solely financed by Alliance mortgages. During the period 1955-60 these 14 companies received mortgages from the Alliance amounting to £1.3 million.

Coleman-Cohen property companies have continued. Their borrowings from the Alliance have not been on such a large scale, although two companies borrowed over £250,000 in the early 1970s. These loans were entered in the society's annual return to members and the chief registrar as special advances to companies in Schedule No. 4 Section B as opposed to Schedule No. 9 Section B, which refers to advances made to a company of which a director of the society (or his nominee) was also a director or shareholder. Technically the Coleman-Cohen companies fall outside such a definition and hence members, the general public at large and the Chief Registrar of Friendly Societies are unlikely to know that the Alliance made very substantial loans to companies connected with the Coleman-Cohen family.

Final remarks

It is clear that, prior to the implementation of preventive legislation, the use of building society funds for property specula-tion by directors and associates was on a huge scale. This is perfectly in line with what one would expect, as expressed in Nichol's theory of 'managerial diversion'. One would not expect otherwise from rational economic people.

The purpose of the new legislation was not to prevent fraud like that at the State; the law in that regard was already satisfactory, the men concerned were gaoled. But the State scandal highlighted the issue, made it a matter of public concern and provoked the rules on special advances: that building societies should not lend large amounts of money to property companies, especially those connected with their directors or their families.

To what extent has legislation concerning special advances changed behaviour? The law limits the amount of special advances that may be made, but as these limits are a percentage of total advances, the amount of money can be huge in a large building society. (See the vast loans made to Villagate Ltd, a small private company.) It is difficult to know how widespread is the sort of behaviour outlined in the cases in this chapter. However, the evidence presented here is the result of only a small research project. It started with an examination of a handful of companies that received special advances from the Alliance during 1980/81. I found that two of these were connected and this triggered off a more intensive search of the Bernard Clarke Group.

But the Britannia's actions suggest that large loans to corporate borrowers are still an important use of building society funds. They have continued to finance the Bernard Clarke group. They have lent huge amounts to the Berger companies, a significant amount of it on property already owned. The Berger companies are the subject of considerable public outrage because of their record as bad landlords.

The extent to which this is typical of other building societies is difficult to assess. It has been shown how the Alliance lent to the Bernard Clarke group, and has financed the Colman-Cohen property companies. The Nationwide has also lent large sums to the Bergers and the Bernard Clarke group.

My examination of some other building societies' annual returns indicated that large loans are sometimes made (quite legally) to building society directors' own firms, and that these are not necessarily for property deals. For example, the Scarborough lent £68,000 in 1981 to G.A. Pindar Ltd, printers. G.T.V. Pindar, a director, is also director of the Scarborough. The Portsmouth lent £70,000 in 1975 and a further £100,000 in 1980 to Spartrucks Ltd, commercial vehicle dealers. D.W. Russell, a director, is also a director of the Portsmouth.

And what of the attitudes to special advances? The BSA is ambivalent. Its official guide to building society finance states: 'The limitation on special advances restricts the scope for undesirable lending.'[16] But Mark Boleat, deputy secretary of the BSA and their main spokesperson said, 'If the law says it is all right, it cannot be undesirable.'[17]

9. Relations with other professionals

Previous chapters have shown how the motivations of building society managers have determined the oligopolistic/monopolistic policies of the building societies. Like other business people they maximize their personal benefits in income, wealth, power, prestige and status. However they are constrained by the non-profit motive — they cannot share directly in the societies' financial success. But often building societies are only one of a business person's interests. The directorship of a building society would be most useful for widening the range of business contacts. Monopolistic power is not simply a matter of dominating a particular industry but also involves the control of the auxillary businesses. This chapter looks at building societies as part of the whole housing provision process —involving builders, solicitors, estate agents and so on — and at the way in which they are controlled by other parts of the property world.

These aspects of monopolistic behaviour are recognized in Britain. In the late seventies the building societies were widely criticized for the practice of asking a borrower to insure with a nominated insurance company. In 1979, at the instigation of the Office of Fair Trading, the BSA recommended to its members that existing borrowers be given the right to choose their insurance company. (New borrowers had had a choice since 1975.)

The fight against monopoly is an unequal battle. Government bodies, such as the Monopolies Commission and the Office of Fair Trading, have quite limited powers. They face enormous economic forces within industries. To some extent monopolistic effects, whether in the form of restrictive practices or others, are an inevitable result of our current form of economic organization.

Chapter 1 gave some indication of how this works in the

building societies. The National Consumer Council drew attention to the monopoly enjoyed by the exchange professionals and to the interconnections between building society managers, surveyors, estate agents, accountants, solicitors, builders and others, reinforced by the positions held by some of these people on town councils and other bodies. These professionals have considerable control over 'the property transaction' in that they are directly involved at each stage. One person, or a small group of persons with 'enough fingers in enough pies' will be in a position to determine housing policy and character in a particular area over a period of time —quite legally and even unwittingly. Three examples of these complex relationships are given in this chapter.

The Alliance Building Society

The Alliance Building Society is Britain's eighth largest building society with assets of £2,500 million. Its directors are predominantly executives and ex-executives of the society and important members of the property world.

The chair is C.J. Baker, an actuary who has spent his working life in the insurance world. He has extensive knowledge and experience of property and investment matters. He is a director of the Abbey Life Assurance Co. Ltd and Hampton Gold Mining Areas Ltd, and is also chair of the Hunting Gate Group, the Victory Insurance Co. Ltd and the Property Unit Trusts Group. The Pension Fund Property Unit Trusts Group, of which he is also chair, has assets of £250 million and offers investors, such as pension funds, units of investment in all types of property, mainly in London and the South of England.

Other directors include R.H. Braybon, managing director of T.J. Braybon & Son Ltd, a large private firm of building contractors and developers in Brighton, and B.P. Graves, senior partner of Graves, Son and Pilcher, a Brighton firm of surveyors, valuers, auctioneers and estate agents. (When I inquired in mid-1981, Graves, Son and Pilcher were the sole agents for the Braybon houses currently on sale).

The remaining directors are R.M. Leadley, who retired from the society in 1979; Howard Johnson, a solicitor and former Brighton

MP; Professor M.W. Thompson, Vice-Chancellor of the University of East Anglia; Lord Hankey, a retired diplomat; Leslie Farrer-Brown, a retired barrister; Roy Cox, chief general manager; and M.C. Griffiths, deputy chief general manager.

R.H. Coleman-Cohen retired from the Alliance board in April 1982. He had been a director of the society since 1946. His retirement ended the Coleman-Cohen family's strong relationship with the Alliance over many decades (see chapter 8). R.H. Coleman-Cohen was also an insurance broker and a partner in a large firm of surveyors and estate agents in Brighton.

The Alliance relies heavily on its professional connections and agents as sources of funds. It also provides them with finance. In 1979 and 1980 the society made 25 special advances to companies. Most of these were to professional firms such as insurance brokers, estate agents and business transfer agents. One loan was to a domestic appliances shop and three loans were to property companies, two of these within the Bernard Clarke and Partners Group of Companies (see Chapter 8).

I asked Mr Roy Cox, the general manager of the Alliance, about this and he stated that these special advances were either for property companies, as part of the Alliance's policy of 'total housing', or for offices operated as agencies conducting society business (although this does not explain the advances made to the domestic appliances shop even though the premises were previously owned by the society and the mortgage provided so as to obtain the highest price).

But this is only part of the picture. Professionals such as firms of solicitors, accountants, surveyors, architects, and financial consultants are usually partnerships rather than companies so even if money has been lent to them they do not come into the special advances category. There is no public information on the total amount of this kind of lending.

As this example shows building societies do not lend money solely for the promotion of home ownership. They are part of the wider world of property business in which property men and exchange professionals comprise their boards, and by which property companies, and many other types of business, are financed.

Special advances

In 1980 I undertook a study of special advances. Most societies do not lend up to the maximum amount allowed for special advances — the Lion and State cases are exceptional. (However, the Peckham Mutual's auditors report for 1980 drew attention to the fact that it had exceeded the special advances limitations for that year; and the major reason for the closure of the New Cross was that it exceeded those limits during 1982.)

In my sample of 57 building societies for the years 1979 and 1980, 27 societies gave no advances to directors and their companies. Out of the total, 46 gave no, or a very few, special advances. This was particularly so in the case of small societies. Eleven out of 17 small societies in the sample made no special advance to companies. Two of the remaining small societies made nearly the maximum amount allowed by law.

The study confirmed the view that although such special advances may be a small proportion of the total funds as far as the individual firms were concerned, these could still be considerable.

The case of Leeds Permanent and James Miller and Partners is outstanding. James Miller and Partners Limited are Edinburgh's biggest landlords. In 1982 they borrowed £170,000; in 1981 £112,000, in 1980 £465,000; in 1979, £398,000 in 1978, £338,000, and in earlier years even more. *The Economist* took this matter up. 'Why should an Edinburgh company get such a huge share (generally more than 50 per cent and in 1977, more than 95 per cent) of a Yorkshire building society's rationed corporate lending? For "historic" reasons says Leeds Permanent.'[1]

In the field of building finance it is particularly common to find a few companies getting most of a society's special advances, despite the strong traditional opposition to this, as a result of the collapse of the Liberator Building Society at the end of the last century.

The Halifax usually provides over £100,000 each year to Shepherd Homes Ltd (£186,000 in 1982; £123,000 in 1981; £133,000 in 1980).

The Abbey National provides funds for Wates Ltd, (£1,667,000 owing at the end of 1982), Kas Construction (£481,000 in 1980 and

£564,000 in 1978) and Ryford Homes (£607,000 in 1982 and £775,000 in 1980).

The construction companies that are fortunate enough to obtain building society finance are usually those with large land banks. They will often own enough land for many years' worth of building at current rates.

A Community Development Project (CDP) was most critical of the practice of land-banking, arguing that it benefited the land bank companies but not home buyers. A smooth supply of land neither ensured a smooth supply of new houses nor did it produce lower priced, better houses. It simply resulted in additional profits being made out of property speculation: the companies concerned would buy land cheap and wait until the market was ready to sell off houses, as before, at the top of the market. The report states:

> Making sure there's a smooth flow of land for their building operations is certainly one motive, but for many companies, which in effect have a dual function as landowner and house builder, landholding is a significant — and very profitable — side of their operations in its own right.
>
> Smaller companies hold little land and buy what they use with overdraft money, so they aim to complete and sell the houses built in a short time period — perhaps even less than a year. Profits from land speculation are not available to them. They have to make do with the usual small profit margin in house building — around 5% net of the selling price.[2]

In some cases building societies have played a major part in helping companies build up their land bank. Shepherd Homes started life in 1946 as the Cozy Cinema Company, growing quickly as a building company during the 1960s. By 1973 its building land and development services were reckoned to be worth £2,073,406, by 1974, £2,958,526, forming the major part of the company's assets. This stock of 'idle' land was used by Shepherd Homes to raise money, by mortgaging it — sites, plots and half-finished housing too. From 1960 to 1973 they took out 90 mortgages with building societies like the Halifax, Abbey National and Bradford or groups like the Forward Trust, United Dominions Trust or their own Shepherd Pension Fund. Loans like the £165, 595 they were able to raise in 1973–4 from the Halifax Building Society on six acres of empty land in Bridlington, or the £25,875 the Abbey National gave them on a site in Selby are only two of many they got on the strength of the land they held. They were even able to use the pension contributions of their own employees to advantage by borrowing from the Shepherd Group Pension Trust.[3] The CDP concluded:

> For the bigger developer-builders the land bank is an important source of funds. But for those who need a home, land-banking means that they have to pay even higher prices when the property market is booming, while in slump they see houses left unfinished, find them finished below standard or not available at all. Meanwhile their own pension contributions or building society savings may well be going to fuel the very process that makes it impossible for them to find somewhere to live.[4]

My study also confirmed that some societies lent companies large sums — quite within the law — secured on commercial and office premises. In addition to those mentioned in chapter 8, in 1980 the Provincial lent £125,000 to Thames Valley Secretariat Ltd, a secretarial agency, and the Guardian in 1979 lent £90,000 to Coolmona Ltd, both for office accommodation. Loans to clubs include those by the Bristol and West to the Knowle Golf Club (£5,000) and the Bourne Club, Farnham (£20,000) in 1979. Additionally, the Bradford and Bingley recently granted a mortgage to the Olicana Bridge Club, in which a director of the Bradford and Bingley had a major interest (as defined by Part 5, Section G of the 1983 annual return).

The sample showed that advances to directors are large and frequent, relative to the number of directors. Most of these loans are personal mortgages secured on their homes. Of the 57 societies in my sample about half did not grant loans to directors during the 1979–80 analysis period. Of the other half there were 36 new loans during the period. As building society directors are almost always very old men (see chapter 12) this is rather surprising. Many of these mortgages are subsequent 'topping up' finance.

Loans to directors' companies are less frequent. Examples

include: the Portsmouth's and the Scarborough's (see page 106); the Nationwide's £75,000 loan to 'The Industrial Society', a management training and advisory company of which Leonard Williams is a director. He is also a director and chief general manager of the Nationwide. (The Industrial Society is incorporated under the 1948 Companies Act but has no share capital.)

Perhaps the most controversial special advances concern the Anglia, which were made the subject of a 'Watchdog' feature on BBC's *Nationwide* in May 1982. This revealed that

> over the last 15 years a total of 12 loans had been made to a company associated with chartered accountants Thornton Baker . . . a firm in which Anglia's Chairman, Jack Corin, is a senior partner. For example, £68,500 was lent on a property at Castilian Street Northampton, £100,000 on premises in Kettering. Again, in 1980, a further £100,000 went on the Thornton Baker premises in Wellingborough. Altogether a total of £373,500 was advanced to Thornton Baker Nominees Ltd.[5]

Nationwide asked Anglia's Chair, Jack Corin, if there was a conflict of interest between his role as a building society chair and his role as a senior partner in Thornton Baker. He replied:

> No, no. The only aspect of lending there are the normal ones that the building society does to any individual or any one of its agents. It has always been our policy at the Anglia and in any such occasion when such a loan might be considered the Board know that I am an interested party in the matter.[5]

Actually there was a slight discrepency. A loan to Thornton Baker Nominees in 1976 for £6,000 was not reported in the Anglia's annual return to the Registrar of Friendly Societies. This was acknowledged as a slip and accepted by the chief registrar as a 'genuine mistake'. Thornton Baker are not agents of the society.

The Tyne & Wear connection

The CDP Information and Intelligence Unit unearthed an instructive case study of the interlocking connections between professionals concerned with housing finance, exchange and contruction.

In their introduction to the research report the CDP noted how connections between local government and exchange professionals were used illegally to shape council housing development in the North East.

> Two major features emerge. First is a web of professional connections which directs component services of a property transaction to particular firms. Second, is the integration within this network of finance for tenanted as well as owner-occupied property.[6]

They produce a chart showing interconnected professionals in about 1976.[7] This chart is not reproduced here as it does not specify the nature of many of the connections. It probably remains much the same today although certain firms' names have changed. (The Tyne Commercial Building Society is now the Tyne; Dickinson Miller & Turnbull, solicitors, are now Dickinson Dees & Co; the St Andrews Building Society has been taken over.)

Tyne & Wear has a number of small building societies and the Northern Rock, a much larger society with branches in many other parts of the country and founded by a merger between a number of small societies in the area, has its head office in Newcastle. The CDP concentrated on the North Shields societies (the Tynemouth, Tynemouth Victoria, Standard, and Mercantile). It was reported that 'these societies have a total of thirty directors. These include five solicitors, two estate agents, two builders and five accountants.' Since then the situation has changed very little. The CDP continue:

> Exchange professionals depend on connections like these to get business. Estate agents make money selling a house and a buyer is much easier to find if they can arrange building society finance. Solicitors depend on new clients for a substantial part of their conveyancing work and it helps if they are recommended by estate agents or can themselves arrange building society finance. Building societies need investors and it helps if solicitors channel trust funds their

way. Agency arrangements in North Shields bear this out. In all, the local societies have thirteen agents in Newcastle, Whitley Bay and Wallsend. Of these agencies five are held by estate agents or legal partnerships which either include a building society director or close relative of a building society director.[8]

Take the Dickinson family. R.H. Dickinson is a director of the Northern Rock Building Society and many limited companies. (One of these, Northumberland & Durham Properties Ltd, received a £120,000 special advance from the Northern Rock in 1972). Some of these companies are very large: for example, the Grainger Trust and the Hume Investment Trust, one of whose subsidiaries is Target Life Assurance. Dickinson is also senior partner in Dickinson Dees, a firm of Newcastle solicitors. I.J. Dickinson is also a partner and a director of the Grainger Trust. The Grainger Trust borrowed money from the Rock Permanent (now Northern Rock) Building Society, its official solicitors are Dickinson Dees, and its registered office is at the same address.[9] The Dickinsons have other common directorships, for example, Broadpool Property and Investment Company. Dickinson Dees are the official solicitors for William Leech (Builders) plc, and two of its partners are also directors. Northern Homes and Estates are a large property company and estate agents in the area, and a subsidiary of William Leech (Builders) plc. J.W.N. Petty, a partner in Dickinson Dees, is a director of both companies. R.F. Walker, also with Dickinson Dees, is a director of Gateshead Land and Property.

Focusing on another part of the 'web', F.B. Hindmarsh and Partners, surveyors, are secretaries of the Seaton Trust (at the same address) whose principal activity is 'the letting of freehold dwelling houses, flats, shops and lock-up garages'. A.B. Hindmarsh and E.D. Jetterson are two of the directors. Mr Jetterson is also a director of the Tynemouth Building Society. Hindmarsh and Partners are agents for the Tynemouth BS.

Turning to the Standard Building Society, two of its directors are also directors of Camden Estates (North Shields). The last time this company received special advances from the Standard was in 1975.

A director of the Mercantile Building Society is D. Burton, a building contractor and director of Collinwood Estates Ltd and F. Fades Ltd. Both of these companies received special advances from the Mercantile during the 1970s.

The Chislehurst connection

The previous case study looked at the involvement of property men, exchange professionals and building societies in housing finance in a particular area.

Here we focus on Hollington Court, Chislehurst, at one time the centre of a network of interconnected finance businesses, a building society, property development companies, estate agents and insurance agents, and extending to large property companies traded on the London Stock Exchange, Lloyds Brokerage, and a London casino. The origins are the Thrush family and the Lion Building Society. (The case of the Lion and the Bernard Clarke Group of Companies was examined in the previous chapter, where certain illegalities concerning the Lion were reported. It is not correct to infer any illegalities in the present case, which merely demonstrates the nature of the interlocking businesses in the property world.)

The web of interconnections is shown in figure 4. Dots indicate directorships, major shareholdings, partnerships or management of the Lion Building Society branch at Hollington Court. No indication is given in the figure of the time span of any connection nor whether any of them are contemporaneous: the dots simply indicate material interests during the period from the early 1960s to the early 1980s.

By the beginning of the 1960s the Thrush family, together with J.S. Brain and H.D. Leyland-Barton had established the Lion, the Universal Mercantile Bank and Colin Gray and Co., estate agents and auctioneers, in the three ground floor office frontages in the new block of offices and flats at Hollington Court. They also had interests in property construction and ownership companies, such as Colin Gray (Contracts) Ltd, which were often financed by the Lion. The Thrush family developed and diversified their interests. Much later Langford, Beavis and de Maid joined Colin Gray and

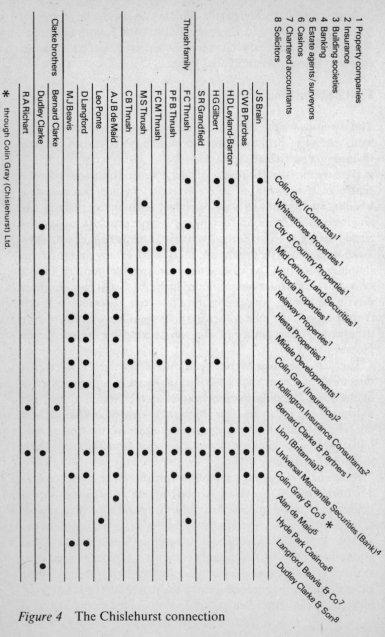

Figure 4   The Chislehurst connection

Co., and the Thrushes, Brain and Leyland-Barton eventually withdrew.

A major partnership developed between F.C. Thrush and Dudley Clarke, also brother of Bernard Clarke, and a solicitor practising from the prestigious address of 6 Hobart Place, SW1. Dudley Clarke also had an interest in the Universal Mercantile Bank. Around this time they acquired two dormant property companies and turned them into major public companies traded on the London Stock Exchange, City and Country Properties and Victoria Property and Investment Ltd, which both operated, first from 25 Harley Street, then from 11 Hobart Place. Growth was enormous. The Thrush/Clarke interest in Victoria ceased around 1965 and it was eventually taken over by Westmoreland Properties. The interest in City and Country probably continued until 1969 when it was taken over by William Stern and became a major part of the Freshwater Group.

The Thrush family and their partners had many other related business interests. Insurance brokerage at Hollington Court was conducted through Colin Gray (Insurance) Ltd, and Hollington Insurance Consultants Ltd. Elsewhere the Thrush family had many other insurance interests and F.C. Thrush was a Lloyds underwriter.

Another interesting partnership involves Leo Poute, a director and major shareholder of Hyde Park Casinos, owners of the Park Lane Casino Club (later to lose its licence and closed in December 1979) and of whom F.C. Thrush was a director. Until recently Capt. Leo Ponte was a director of Universal and Mercantile. Ladbrokes took over Hyde Park Casinos and Leo Ponte resigned his directorship in 1976. Sir Demond Heap, a director of the Britannia at the time, became a director of Hyde Park Casinos in October 1979.

Universal and Mercantile Bank lent to the Thrush property companies in the normal course of business. In 1980 it changed its name to Universal and Mercantile Securities. Its directors still are members of the Thrush family and its business is 'banking, receiving funds on current and deposit accounts, and applying them for the purposes of loans and investments'. The last accounts submitted to Companies House at the end of December 1983 were those to 31 August 1980, although the auditors, Simmons Cohen Fine and Partners, served until 1 August 1982. In their audit report dated 3 July 1974 on the August 1971 accounts, Turquands Barton Mayhew & Co. stated: 'certain weaknesses in accounting controls have arisen in the company's Cashmaster division and an indemnity has been given in respect of any unrecorded liabilities.' Turquands later became part of Ernst and Whinney. After their audit of the August, 1978 accounts, Ernst and Whinney did not seek re-election.

The 1980s have seen the separation of control of the three offices on the front of Hollington Court — the Britannia BS, Universal Mercantile Securities, and Colin Gray & Co., estate agents — mainly because of the age of the people involved. Grandfield and Purchas have now retired from the Britannia, the Thrush interest in Colin Gray & Co. seems to have been bought out; Messrs Langford and Beavis, who have a chartered accountancy practice in a side office in Hollington Court, now have a major interest.

Final remarks

This chapter tells of something well-known in the building society world and its related professions. Its dangers are also recognized. To quote a recent *Guardian* editorial:

> The small societies have always posed the problem of supervising potential conflicts of interest and straight impropriety where local estate agents, builders, solicitors and surveyors control funds available for new and second-hand housing and have local information that they can combine to personal benefit.[10]

However, this chapter, and to some extent the previous one, lead us to believe that such potential problems do not only apply to the small societies. It must be asked how many more branches are there within large societies that have origins like the Lion's? There must be some. Many of the 'rogue' societies mentioned in chapter 8 were taken over in much the same way as the Lion.

The major point of this chapter concerns the 'business culture' of the property world of which building societies are part. The boards of directors of building societies invariably comprise exchange professionals and property men (see table 19). According to *The Economist* most of the directors of the 20 largest societies are non-executive and almost every society has only one executive

Table 19 What building society directors do

Company director (mostly property companies)	59
Building society executive	27
Surveyor	26
Retired	23
Accountant	22
Solicitor	20
Consultant	10
Farmer	3
Miscellaneous	24
Undisclosed	13
Total	**227**

Source: Annual returns of 20 largest building societies, 1982

on the board.[11] (The Halifax is an exception with four.) Invariably the directors have property interests. The Alliance, cited as an example here, is a major society and of the highest repute. Both R.H. Coleman-Cohen and Lord Cohen of Brighton held very high offices at the BSA.

The feeling of dissatisfaction and unease with what is regarded as 'good practice' was forcibly expressed in the conclusions of the CDP report on the housing finance system:

Written out of 4 years work in some of the poorest parts of Britain's major cities *Profits against Houses* describes a system which operates in every corner of the country. A system which the government supports by allowing it to continue, forcing workers to pay ever more for their homes. While public expenditure cuts mean fewer council houses and local authority mortgages, the government's long awaited review of Housing Finance drags on. When it finally reports it will undoubtedly only tinker with details leaving the system unchanged — this report shows how no amount of tinkering will improve the harsh conditions in the CDP areas and the many others like them.

Perhaps because of this *Profits against Houses* will be one of our last inter-project reports. Set up by the government to take part in the tinkering now CDP's voice, the Information and Intelligence Unit, is being closed down. The state sent us in, this is what we found, so it is shutting us up.[12]

10. Fraud and other irregularities

This chapter considers the ultimate and illegal form of 'managerial diversion' — the misappropriation of funds by employees. It also extends the discussion of mergers in chapter 6 by questioning whether the small building society is a sound unit (if not, presumably it should be taken over). It examines other irregularities where no fraud or dishonesty was involved.

The thesis is this: the traditional small society is prone to misappropriation and dishonest use. It may be a vehicle for raising funds for its directors' other interest, or because of its size, there are inadequate controls to safeguard its funds from avaricious and dishonest managers. However the large society is not necessarily without risk; computer fraud is well-known, and a largely non-executive board of directors may be impotent to control all the policies and practices of a large society.

Are building societies prone to, and bad at dealing with fraud? Building societies seem to have a high propensity for misappropriations. The 1970s witnessed three major frauds, at the Wakefield, the Grays, and the Alfreton. They stimulated both the action and antagonism of the BSA, the Chief Registrar of Friendly Societies, and the Institute of Chartered Accountants (ICA). The Inspectors investigating the Grays affair were most critical of the BSA, and particularly concerned about some general aspects of the financial controls of small societies.

Let us first trace the developments of the Wakefield, Grays and Alfreton scandals.

The Wakefield

With assets of £24 million the Wakefield Building Society was 'considered to be eminently sound and capably managed'.[1] In fact two of its managers had recently been on the council of the BSA and were actively involved in the Yorkshire District branch of the BSA and the Building Societies Institute.

The chief registrar reports:

> On 30 June 1976 representatives of the Wakefield Building Society reported that the audit for year ended 31 March 1976, conducted by newly appointed auditors, had revealed that certain advances previously regarded by the society as mortgages were not supported by appropriate deeds and advance records. The resulting losses and overstatement of assets were initially estimated to be in the region of £600,000 and had accumulated over a period of more than 20 years. The society's General Manager and Secretary, Mr. W. Robinson, had been suspended from duty.
>
> The losses and overstatement of assets in due course estimated from the accounts of the Wakefield amounted to £663,190 including accumulated interest of £388,487. These sums included advances (together with interest thereon) to a former general manager of the Wakefield, the late Mr. G.E. Jackson. I understand that legal action is being taken which if successful could lead to recovery of a substantial sum from the G.E. Jackson Will Trust Fund of which Mr. W. Robinson is sole trustee.[2]

Robinson was over 70 and had been a director since 1954. He was well respected both within building society circles and locally as a worker for charity and a Methodist lay preacher.

Apparently he was able to perpetrate the fraud by having complete control over his subordinates and an auditor who always dealt with him rather than the board of directors of the society:

> This auditor was an elderly man who wanted to resign in 1974 but was persuaded to go on in 1975 to complete 50 years as auditor.[3]

The Wakefield fraud shocked and concerned the Chief Registrar of Friendly Societies. He was forced to ask why in this and other cases misappropriations had gone on for many years without detection. His reaction was to write to all chairs of building societies in 1976 reminding them of their statutory duties as directors concerning the maintenance of adequate controls and records. (See Appendix, The Wakefield letter.)

As it turned out, this was to bring further embarrassment.

The Grays

The Grays affair has all the ingredients of a classic scandal. It can have no better introduction than the first page of the Inspectors' Official Report — usually very stodgy documents:

1. On Friday 17 March 1978, Harold Percy Jaggard, the 79 year-old Chairman and Secretary of the Grays Building Society (the Grays) was found dead in his bath at home. A suicide note, left for his wife, said:

'Do not go to the bathroom alone. For forty years I have tried to put somebody else's misdeeds right and I can take no more. Chapman no blame at all. Be good to my relations. Love H.'

2. This note and the circumstances which immediately preceded Mr. Jaggard's suicide, indicated the possibility of irregularities in the books of the Grays, of which Mr. Jaggard had been acting as Secretary since 25 August 1927. Mrs. Connie Saunders of the auditor's staff had been the first to discover the errors; she was working in the boardroom at the Grays on the Friday in question with Mr. Arthur Nudd, the auditor partner:

'I said "There's something gone wrong here." Mr. Jaggard was sitting at the end of the boardroom table. Mr. Nudd was sitting directly opposite me; and Mr. Jaggard was up by my side straight away before Mr. Nudd even had a chance.'

Mr. Davidson: 'What did he say?'

A: 'He said "Carry on and I'll attend to that later." '

Jerry Fox, the chief cashier, continues the account:

'He must have been upstairs with the auditors. He came downstairs. We heard him come down. He has a distinctive walk. He came out on to the front counter, the part where the clients stand, to go out of the door. He said, "It looks like rain. I'll have to go and get my coat." He did not have his mack with him or hat. We let him back in because the door is controlled by electric working. He came in, put his hat and coat on and said, "I won't be long. I'll be about 20 minutes." That was about 20 past 12, and he never came back.'

3. With Mr. Jaggard's continued and inexplicable absence that afternoon and the evidence discovered by Mrs. Saunders, the staff became alarmed. Mr. George Chapman, the Assistant Secretary, and Mr. Nudd carried out certain initial checks and late that evening news of Mr. Jaggard's death reached them. Mr. Nudd telephoned Mr. Peter Dowson the senior London partner of Appleby, English & Partners, the auditors, on the Friday night. The following day, Mr. Nudd, Mr. Dowson and Mr. John Walter, an Assistant Registrar from the Registry of Friendly Societies (the Registry) attended a hastily summoned meeting of the board of directors of the Grays. Mr Dowson's notes record:

'1. Absolute discretion be exercised to ensure no "public" knowledge of possible difficulties which might result in a panic affecting the building society movement as a whole.

2. That urgent representations be made to the Building Societies Association with a view to support from another member society with regards management, personnel and (if necessary) finance with view to merger. Mr. Walter undertook to process this as a matter of urgency.

3. The auditors would attempt to quantify the probable total of the financial problem (if indeed there was one) as quickly as possible.'

It was agreed that the society's offices would be opened as usual the following Monday to avoid unnecessary public reaction.[4]

The society's assets were stated at £10 million but it transpired that Jaggard's applications amounted to £2 million, plus £5 million in interest. It was estimated that Jaggard's betting lost £1.6 million. The defalcations dated back as far as 1938.

Jaggard was married three times, and between 1942 and 1960 was supporting two households. The Inspectors write:

> It is clear that this must have placed a considerable strain upon his finances, or to be more precise, upon the finances of Grays. During this period Mr. Jaggard sent John Jaggard and Francis Giles to private school. The children of both households had occasional continental holidays. Although neither household was run with ostentatious extravagance, we are satisfied that both families lived comfortably. Mr. Jaggard himself had his suits made at West End tailors; he smoked expensive cigars; he ran two cars and sometimes a third; there were frequent delicacies from Harrods and Fortnums and neither woman lacked cash for spending.[5]

Jaggard was often seen at race meetings with women, and brief cases stuffed with money.

Jaggard's fraud was perpetuated in a similar way to Robinson's at the Wakefield — by completely dominating the office staff and having ineffectual auditors. His technique of 'teaming and lading' is well known and involved covering up his thefts by accelerating the banking of cheques received in a later accounting period. Cheques used to cover the thefts were usually those for the repayment of mortgages but also included cheques received from investors. For the year-end accounts, he would simply take the summary books home and forge the necessary entries. That he could do this for over 40 years without anyone ever suspecting is truly amazing.

But his behaviour and regular attendance at race meetings did arouse some tittering comment. The board of directors instigated an investigation by the auditors, but they found things to be in order.

Who, and what, can be blamed for all this? The answer lies in the story of events following the Registry's reaction to the Wakefield's collapse. Jaggard duly received 'The Wakefield letter' (reminding directors of their duty to ensure their proper books were kept). None of the directors could recall the letter having been read out even though the minutes of the board meetings stated that it had been.

But the Registry had also been taking a special interest in the Grays from 1973. They had noticed that the average age of directors was 74, that the society had sometimes been late in submitting monthly returns and that its liquidity ratio was only just above the statutory minimum. A representative from the Registry visited the society in 1974 and was not greatly impressed with what he saw. The necessary noises were made by Jaggard and the society regarding mechanization of the books and accounts, but there was no intention of introducing such a system.[6] Vollmar, an Assistant Registrar at the Registry stated that 'the old fashioned accounting methods would necessitate consideration of whether Trustee Status could be continued. He stressed that this was no idle threat.'[7] As events turned out, it was. Of the ages of directors, 'Mr. Vollmar described the present position as being almost farcical. Three directors were over 80 years of age, two between 70 and 80 and the remaining four were all over 60. The older members must definitely consider retiring.'[8] (This is not so different from many leading societies: see chapter 12.)

Jaggard turned for comfort and support to Norman Griggs, Secretary-General of the BSA. It was forthcoming. Griggs replied:

the Registry is pushing matters too hard. Although the Chief Registrar does have an overriding authority to revoke designation (even if the arithmetical requirements are met) it seems unlikely to us that he would do so in your case.

We suggest that you make an effort to build up your Society's liquidity so that you have more latitude above the minimum for trustee status. We also suggest that you do everything possible to bring down the average age of your Board.

If your present accountancy system is working well, there seems no point in the Registry's insistence on further mechanisation.

With regard to a merger with one or both of the other Societies in Grays, we think you should see the implications for the reserve ratio of the new enlarged Society.

Our advice, therefore, is to get your house completely in

order, after which the pressure from the Registry should die down.

Perhaps you would be kind enough to treat this letter in confidence where the Registry is concerned.[9]

The Registry continued to press Jaggard and Griggs continued to support him. In 1976 Griggs wrote to Jaggard that:

it does seem to me that, apart from the liquidity question, he [the Registrar] is probably exceeding his authority.

With regard to your system of book-keeping, the proof of the pudding is in the eating. No complaints about errors ever reach the Association and your management expenses have been kept very low.

My advice would be to play along gently with the Registry on the assumption that they are taking a paternalistic attitude towards your Society rather than one of criticism.

No doubt you will keep this letter confidential as far as the Registry is concerned.[10]

The Registry continued to press for the reforms and instigated another investigation in 1977. These had little effect other than a partial change of directors.

The Inspectors severely criticised the BSA. In its evidence to the Wilson Committee, the BSA described itself as a trade association for member building societies. It said:

The Association regards one of its major roles as being to protect the public and to offer them an information service. The Association closely monitors the accounts of each member-society with a view to ensuring that difficulties do not arise which might jeopardize people's savings. On the very few occasions when societies have run into difficulty the Association has stepped in very quickly to ensure that investors and borrowers are fully protected.[11]

Accordingly the Inspectors considered the attitude of Griggs of the BSA to be 'somewhat misguided' in seeking to defend Grays against the Registry 'without at any rate having available appropriate information upon which to judge the merits of the case'.[12]

At that stage the BSA had made no investigation into how the Grays was run or how its accounting system operated. In fact the Inspectors criticize the BSA for not conducting a proper investigation.

Peter Wilkinson (at that time general manager of the Anglia) was asked by Griggs to go and have a look at the Grays in 1977. The visit, which 'lasted about an hour and a half' was made in order to get a general picture of the place and to speak to Mr Jaggard and Mr Chapman, the assistant secretary, with whom he spoke alone.[13] Wilkinson wrote a report to the BSA of his investigation (of which the Inspectors remark, 'if in fact it can be called that').[14] His conclusion was:

> From the evidence on my brief visit I can see no cause for criticism or concern. The working of the Society appears to be well delegated and controlled. Mr. Jaggard is proud of his Society and the service it provides to the area. He does not want to consider the possibility of a merger with another society and does not consider this to be necessary.[15]

The Inspectors also made some major recommendations. The first concerns the duties and responsibilities of building society directors. The report suggests that they should be made fully aware of their duties to ensure that the society keeps proper books of accounts and a proper system of control and inspection of them under Section 76 of the Building Societies Act 1962. The Inspectors suggest that new directors attend a short course on such matters and that existing directors attend refresher courses.

The Inspectors also advise that building society law be brought into line with company law whereby directors are required to resign and seek annual re-election upon reaching the age of 70.

The Inspectors were also concerned that Jaggard abused and exploited his dominant position as chief executive of Grays. They proposed two measures to avoid the repetition of such a situation. The first was that a building society chair should never, at the same time, be the chief executive. The second was that there be at least two executive directors on every board who are familiar with the operations of the society (as in the example of the Alliance in chapter 9).

The Inspectors also made recommendations that the powers of inspectors appointed under the Building Societies Act should be brought in line with the Companies Acts. These are largely technical matters, but they should be noted in connection with the points made in the next two chapters that the new Building Societies Act needs to conform with certain elements of company law.

The other major recommendation concerned building society auditors. They are subject to more stringent requirements than those required of auditors under the Companies Acts. They are obliged to form an opinion on the system of internal control. In the words of the Inspectors: 'we believe . . . that the reason for this lies in Parliament's intention that a higher duty of care should be placed upon those concerned with taking deposits from the public and holding assets on behalf of depositors and upon their statutorily appointed auditors.'[16] They made the following recommendations, therefore:

> that the law be changed so that the Registry may call for the auditor's working papers if appropriate;
> that the auditor's report be extended to state whether proper books had been kept, whether a satisfactory system of internal control was in existence, that they had reported to the directors in writing on the society's accounting and internal control and whether they had attended the meeting of directors at which the annual accounts were approved.

Although these were largely matters involving a change in the law, the Institute of Chartered Accountants wrote to all building society auditors reminding them of their full duties, and the Chief Registrar wrote to *all chairs* (not all directors) reminding them of the duties of all directors.

There then followed the Alfreton scandal.

The Alfreton

The Alfreton was a small society with assets of £6 million, a staff of four and no branch offices. Irregularities were discovered in late 1980. The secretary, Mr Ward, was sentenced on charges of theft, false accounting and forgery. The fraud had been going on since at least 1975 and amounted to £191,072.

The chair of the Alfreton was J.N. Flanders FCA. Because of his qualification and experience, he was appointed chair when the society was granted trustee status. He had been suspicious of Ward since 1976 when two other directors told him that Ward appeared to be enjoying a standard of living above what might be expected from his society salary. There was no clear-cut evidence, but Flanders asked the auditors to carry out a 'surprise cash count'. This further aroused his suspicions and he asked the auditors to extend their tests at the next audit, in 1976. They did so, but this revealed nothing. He continued his search to ascertain whether Ward really was living beyond his means.[17] Apparently Flanders was further alerted and requested more checks by the auditors, but because of misunderstandings these were not carried out.[18] In December 1980 Flanders heard that two £5,000 cheques drawn on the society had been paid into Ward's bank account. The auditors were contacted and started an investigation. Within a few hours they had discovered four suspicious cheques amounting to £20,330 which were subsequently found to be fraudulent.

The Alfreton scandal is significant not because of the scale of the fraud but because it occurred in the wake of the Grays affair. The report of a committee of inquiry spoke in a very disparaging and alarming way about small societies generally:

> The difficulties of establishing adequate systems of control and inspection in a small society were, and are still, not generally recognised . . . it should be assumed by all those bearing responsibility — the directors, the auditors, and the Registrar — that small societies, perhaps those with a staff of eight or fewer, cannot meet the internal control and inspection provisions of the Act unless they take special measures to enable them so to do . . . In the light of the large number of small building societies there is a serious danger that some present societies may not have systems to prevent or detect fraud of the type carried out against the Alfreton[19]

These remarks (or findings) must be seen in the context of the purpose of the investigation 'that facts and matters concerning the affairs of the Alfreton . . . may indicate that members of the Institute may have become liable to disciplinary action.[20] The 'Institute' is the Institute of Chartered Accountants of England and Wales and the 'members' are primarily Flanders and the auditors. The committee exonerated these by blaming small building societies and no disciplinary action was taken against them:

> were it not for the Committee's view that there are inherent difficulties in maintaining an adequate system of internal control in small building societies, the lack of a watertight system at the Alfreton might have caused it to criticise more severely those under enquiry.[21]

This provoked a backlash from the BSA, not least because they had already been criticized by one accountant's report — that concerning the Grays. As reported in the *Sunday Telegraph:*

> 'The horrid and unjustified implication of the accountants' report is that these small societies are unsuitable to exist', thundered Richard Weir, secretary-general of the BSA.
> 'It is a wild generalisation based only on the events at Alfreton, where professional accountants showed gross negligence. We will be writing to all the accountancy bodies about this.[22]

The allegations of 'gross negligence' by the accountants involved had no substance; they were contrary to the committee's findings and were not pursued.

The Alfreton was later taken over by the Britannia.

Other irregularities

It should not be thought that these were the only scandals. Some quite extraordinary events led to the takeover of the Tunstall in 1971, by the Leek & Westbourne, later the Britannia. In late 1970 the Britannia had to lend the Tunstall £500,000 as the Tunstall was concerned that it might be unable to honour its obligations to investors and potential borrowers. This followed the discovery that substantial sums had been misappropriated, by the Star

Mutual Permanent Building Society whose merger it had accepted without knowing the true position. The person responsible for the fraud at the Star Mutual was sentenced to four years imprisonment with charges of theft, embezzlement and falsification of accounts over a number of years.[23]

In other cases, while there was no fraud or dishonesty, quite alarming irregularities were discovered. For example, the Chorley (assets £1 million) was taken over by the Bradford and Bingley in 1978, following discovery of a £46,000 discrepancy in the Chorley's accounts.[24] In 1981 the Kingston (assets £20 million) was taken over by the London & South of England, following discovery of irregularities totalling £110,576.[25]

In 1974 the Chief Registrar issued an order controlling the activities of the small Copthall Building Society 'whose business was considered to have been conducted principally for the furtherance of the interests of its directors and in disregard both of the provisions of the 1962 Act and of the interests of potential investors'.[26]

The London & Midland, a small London society, was taken over by the London Goldhawk (later to become the London & South of England) in 1979. This followed the 1978 auditor's report to London & Midland members stating that 'In our opinion the Society has failed to maintain a satisfactory system of control and inspection over its transactions and records as required by Section 76 of the Building Societies Act 1962.' A note attached to the accounts showed 'other management expenses' to include 'provisions in the sum of £6,977 for losses arising on unauthorised loans and cash shortages'.

It should not be inferred from these examples that such dangers are prevalent only at smallish societies. In 1980 the London & South of England called in the police following the discovery of irregularities regarding the priority of mortgage applications. The mortgages were completed by members of staff at the old London Goldhawk, which merged the same year with the South of England to become the London & South of England. It was later announced that no losses were anticipated as a result of the irregularities and that certain members of the society's staff had resigned.[27]

In the meantime, irregularities at small societies still come to light. A discrepancy of £17,700 was discovered at the small Blythe and Morpeth in 1982. The Northern Rock had to provide management support until it could take over.

Final remarks

It should be pointed out that the frauds and other irregularities did not cause loss of funds by members. The societies concerned were taken over and a voluntary compensation fund was arranged. A permanent but voluntary scheme is now in operation.

However the solution of merger has its problems. Given the legal requirements concerning the amount of reserves to be kept by a society, a small number of small societies can be absorbed, but not so the larger ones. With reserves being carried at a small proportion of total assets, losses of £7 million or so, as at Grays, are equivalent to the elimination of a £100 million society.

The story of the Wakefield, the Grays, and the Alfreton shows that small societies have a propensity for fraud and that this is recognized, even though the view of the accountants' committee of inquiry — that all societies with staff of eight or fewer are vulnerable — may be going rather too far.

But it should be remembered that fraud may not be confined to the very small societies. We are led to believe that computer fraud is the modern and rapidly expanding crime.[28] In addition, another kind of problem exists for the large societies. To quote from an article about these matters:

Nor do large societies kid themselves that they are on top of all the criminals even with the massive control paraphernalia they have now built up in response to cases of deception which have recently come to light. The Provincial, based in Bradford, was taught a lesson by a clerk in its Gloucester office. A large number of accounts were tampered with. Depositors and mortgagors were told formally that in the case of any discrepancy noted in the figures for outstanding balances forward to them, they should contact the auditor direct. None ever did. The auditor had, therefore, to set up his own direct verification procedure to be sure of a positive reaction to any obvious discrepancies. It would, of course, be optimistic to expect the average building society member to run straight to the auditor without checking first with branch officials, which removes the point of the exercise.

Societies are highly individualistic in the way they conduct and administer their business. Provincial accepts that all transactions assume some component of trust. Watertight security is an unobtainable dream. Solicitor's clerks, for example, bent on mischief but writing on their firms' notepaper, can extract title deeds from societies without question, and have done so.[29]

In the same way that fraud in the small society places great responsibility and pressure on directors, the more sophisticated computer crime that may be expected in any large financial institution demands of its directors an equally sophisticated response. These matters are discussed in chapter 12.

11. Members *versus* directors

The themes of this book come to a head in the relationship between society members, or shareholders, and directors. Building societies belong to the private sector of the UK economy and are thus self-regulating within a legislative framework which lays down the rights and duties of members and directors. All the problems and policies of the organization are intended to be sorted out within a set of rules focused on the conduct and procedures of members' meetings. A very similar philosophy also applies to companies, and even to partnerships. Transcending this system is a regulator: in the case of building societies, the Chief Registrar of Friendly Societies; and in the case of companies, the Registrar of Companies. Their duties are to ensure that the necessary public returns and accounts are made and that the law is obeyed. They have special powers of investigation and, with the co-operation of the courts, issue orders when things go wrong.

One theme of this book is the separation of ownership (members) and control (managers) and their separate and different interests and objectives. One need only assume the most obvious of motives and interests to identify these. Nichols put it: 'The problem facing management in the mutual is the conversion of its power into personal gain of some form.'[1] A second theme is the assumption of natural economic forces: monopolistic and/or ologopolistic positions created and exploited by building society managers, given their natural motivations. A third theme is the set of values, assumptions and expectations adopted by society: that home ownership is 'a good thing', and that it can only be achieved by those who operate the housing system in a certain integrated and exclusive way, whereby monopoly profits are assured.

On the other hand, the public relations of building societies claim mutuality, and the law assumes the same thing. It is significant that the regulator is known as the Chief Registrar of *Friendly Societies*.

To sum up: the manifestations of managerial motives in branch proliferation, excessive management costs, non-economic mergers, red lining, mortgage queue jumping, fraud, diversion of funds, and imprudent financing, will eventually be confronted by investors who will say that it is unacceptable — even though they may acknowledge that it is predictable and, in a way, inevitable.

Such a conflict will occur in members' meetings and other procedures. However, given its assumption of mutuality, the law provides a set of arguably inappropriate rules and procedures to cope with this conflict, together with a regulator of questionable powers.

If this is so, what improvements can be made? First we look at a case involving conflict between members and managers. We then examine company law, to find how unnecessary conflict and undesirable practices can be eliminated.

Democracy in action: C.F.J. Punt *v* the Nationwide

The Nationwide's rules and procedures are probably not very different from those of most other building societies. But for some reason, the Nationwide has attracted a number of members seeking election to the board. Although the society may like to explain this by saying that this demonstrates its democracy, this hardly explains the Nationwide's strange propensity. One can only speculate; perhaps its change of name from the 'Co-operative Permanent' in 1970 was seen by some of its members as indicative of a policy change with which they did not agree.

The most recent aspirant for election to the board of directors is C.F.J. Punt. Punt's offer is just part of a wider challenge by a group of critics of the Nationwide's policy on a range of matters concerning the society's accountability to members, such as board entertainment, expenses and directors' interests. A *Guardian* editorial put it perfectly:

> The bulk of Mr Punt's resolutions are concerned with making the operation of the Nationwide Building Society more open

and accountable to its members. In this he is touching on the central problem for building societies today . . . The problem is that in practice they are not really responsible to anyone else either . . . If he is not allowed an answer, then pray, who is?[2]

If the law and procedures are inappropriate for the resolution, such a conflict (and Punt is a practising solicitor) is potentially a most interesting piece of action research, promising some indication of the nature of necessary reform.

In autumn 1981 Mr Punt submitted the first of a batch of resolutions for the Nationwide annual general meeting (AGM) to be held in late March the following year. At the same time he requested the necessary forms to enable him to stand as a candidate in the election for directors. The subjects of the resolutions were:

1. That members, and not the board of directors, elect the members of the Regional Boards.
2. That the society must send out for each candidate for office of director a short election address and that the cost of this be paid by the society.
3. That half of the commission received by the society on fire, life or other insurance be credited to the member.
4. That minutes of the AGM and special meetings of the society be accessible to members from the local branch office.
5. That the existing rights of directors to co-opt others as elected directors be restricted.
6. That the number of directors retiring from office in rotation but eligible for re-election be increased.
7. That the rights of the directors to appoint executive directors be reduced and the rights of members to remove them by certain criteria (for example, absenting themselves from board meetings without permission from the board) be increased.
8. Fees of directors to be the subject of a decision at each AGM.

There were also resolutions concerning more trivial matters such as: when the AGM should be held, the provision of further information concerning charitable donations, the provision of rules to new members, notices of members' meetings, the last date for submitting ordinary resolutions at meetings, and the election of meeting scrutineers.

In February 1982 Punt discovered that the Nationwide was to change the system of proxy voting on his resolutions. In previous years the proxy form allowed the member to appoint someone other than a director as proxy and so ensuring voting according to the member's wishes. In the new system, the society named three directors as alternate proxies, leaving no space on the proxy form for the member to insert another name. (In both the old and the new systems the proxy made decisions as the proxy found appropriate.) Punt complained to the society, but to no avail.

Punt therefore decided to take his case to the High Court, seeking an injunction against the use of a system which he considered unfair and, he claimed, contrary to the society's rules. The society denied this allegation. The usual means of dealing with disputes between building societies and their members is provided for in the Building Societies Act 1962, and involves going before the Chief Registrar of Friendly Societies who makes a ruling. Punt chose not to follow this path as it would have been too slow to be of any use: the proxy documents were already being sent to members with the agenda for the AGM. The High Court Judge ruled that he had no jurisdiction to deal with the matter because of the provisions of the 1962 Act which excluded the resolution of these disputes by outside bodies.

So the board's proxy system was used. Punt considered it unfair, as the proxy card sent to all members:

> did not have provision for the proxy to be mandated, nor was there any space, as was usual, for a name to be inserted for an alternative to the establishment proxies to be appointed. Thus the combination of these facts meant that the card could only be used by those content to vote with the establishment.
> There was a note to members at the bottom of the card which advised those wishing to appoint some other person as proxy to change the form for a blank form at any office of the society. Thus were much more stringent conditions imposed on those who wished to vote for the resolutions than on those

content to vote against. Of course, the Act provides that a notice about proxies has to be printed on the agenda for the meeting, and no particular piece of paper has to be used provided the notice is in the correct form, but the fact that cards were supplied tended to give members the idea that only official forms were acceptable.

Before the March AGM the dealings between Nationwide and Punt grew more strained. Punt asked for details of money spent by staff on entertainment in 1981. When the society refused to provide the information, he wrote to the auditors (Touche Ross & Co.) who also refused. He therefore added a further resolution for the AGM proposing that, in view of their refusal, the firm should no longer act as the society's auditors.

Punt also sought to obtain a copy of the society's AR11 (its annual return) prior to the AGM. This was also refused *on the advice of legal counsel* because of the 1962 Act wording which states 'on or after the date . . .' (This policy was reversed for the 1983 AGM. In a memorandum to a board meeting, dated 18 November 1982, Cyril English, chief general manager, wrote: 'It seems that if we continue our past practice it will be technically correct but will not have the sympathy of the Registry or a section, at least, of public opinion.')

Eventually the phrasing of the resolutions were agreed and took the form of 19 special resolutions and two ordinary resolutions (one of which concerned the non-reappointment of the auditors). In the statement to members outlining the special resolutions, the board of directors wrote:

> The board must have serious reservations when wholesale changes are proposed by someone without the necessary knowledge and experience of the affairs of Nationwide Building Society or of building society operations generally.
> The present rules conform to both the spirit and the letter of the law as enacted by the Building Society Acts and have been found sensible, reasonable and practical during a period of great expansion and progress.

Punt considered the reference to him being 'without the necessary knowledge and experience' as strange, since no one from the society had questioned him on his knowledge or experience of building society matters. Certainly the diversionary tactic of criticizing the proposer distracted members from wondering why there was little attempt at reasoned opposition to his proposals.

The statement by the board of directors to members ended with the words:

> The board considers that the adoption of any of these proposals would not be in the best interests of the Society and seeks the support of members to secure the rejection of all these Resolutions. For this purpose members are invited to complete the enclosed form of proxy which should be posted to reach the Secretary . . .

The AGM duly arrived. Expectant press and Nationwide members were not disappointed. *The Guardian* covered the meeting on its front page. Under the headline, 'Rebel shakes society to its foundations,' it read:

> A capacity crowd at an AGM is more than 10 people, and more than 500 turned up . . . Sir Herbert Ashworth (chairman of the Nationwide) seemed shell-shocked by the volleys of points of order, amendments and references back.
>
> 'Most of the talking has been done by the audience' he remarked irritably halfway through his five hour ordeal. 'If we reject the accounts as Mr Punt recommends, what do you expect us to do?' 'Resign' came the cry amid ironic cheers.[3]

There were similar accounts in other papers.

Of course this did not happen; as Punt feared, proxy votes ensured that his first five resolutions were defeated and there was no time left to vote on the others.

Of the AGM and its effects, Punt recalls:

> The general mayhem was such that we accurately predicted that the Chairman would not survive in office to fight another day, and that the Board would have to open discussions with us despite refusing so to do prior to the AGM and opposing the resolution which Buck Taylor put up along these lines. At

the close of the 1982 AGM the Building Society Members Association got off the ground when some of those attending the meeting decided to join with us to do something about the appalling state of affairs revealed . . . In setting up the Building Societies Members Association, we capitalised on the early interest by press releases and writing to each of those who had contacted me before the AGM to evince support for our ideas. By December of 1982 we had enough support to hold the inaugural meeting which agreed a constitution and elected a committee and officers. At that time the membership was about 90 and we are now over the two hundred. On behalf of individual members of the Association we have taken up a number of complaints and suggestions with various societies with varying degrees of success. The tangible achievements have been modest, e.g. the agreement of Alliance now to have proxy forms available in each branch whereas members previously were obliged to send for them to the head office, the achievement of some improvements to the rules at Western Counties. Our hope is that this sort of contact with societies will be accepted, as it was in that society, as helpful rather than interfering. With our present lack of time and resources there will be a limit to what can be achieved immediately, and, for a variety of reasons we have to concentrate on the all-important area of pending legislation. Perhaps our best achievement has been to increase public interest and debate and to provide a focus for those seeking reforms.

By now Punt v Nationwide had its own momentum. He challenged the practice of placing asterisks against the names of those on the ballot paper for election to directorship as 'retiring directors who were eligible for re-election'. He considered that such practice was suggestive to members of who to vote for, since those whom the board considered acceptable were identifiable by this criterion. Punt's arguments were technical and centred on the Nationwide's Rule 61 and on the dispute over whether the directors were eligible for re-election when they had never been elected but co-opted or appointed. The dispute was heard at the Registry of Friendly

Societies. Punt lost and received a £575 bill for counsel's legal fees from the Nationwide. As Punt remarks:

> This has serious implications for the small investor with a genuine grievance. The establishment within a society can use the money of members to fend them off, confident that there will be no personal liability, win or lose. The member, who may well be unversed in the law and unable to afford legal representation is then faced with an array of legal talent for which he may well have to foot the bill. When leading counsel is employed it can be heavy indeed. This is particularly incongruous, given that arbitration proceedings are intended to be relatively informal, particularly in the larger societies where there is 'in house' legal talent to be tapped.

Well before 1983 the Nationwide board of directors had already met to plan how to cope with Punt and his requests for reform. Views of counsel were obtained on a wide range of points of building society law and meetings procedure. The availability of the AR11 prior to the AGM was the only concession, and for strategic reasons. In his memorandum to the board of 18 November 1982, Cyril English wrote:

> It is not recommended that supplies of the AR11 should be available at the door of the meeting even if it has been previously made available to members generally. To do so, it is felt, would imply recognition that the AR11 was a document open for discussion at the meeting. To make the AR11 available to members will, undoubtedly, make the Chairman's task more difficult.

The board were steadfast. At the 1982 AGM, Punt had proposed 19 special resolutions; eight were later withdrawn leaving 11 for the 1983 AGM. However, the society queried the admissibility of two of them and their duty to circulate the preamble to a further eight. The dispute was heard by the Chief Registrar of Friendly Societies before the AGM, but since it could not be resolved, it was sent to the High Court for adjudication.

However, the 1983 AGM could scarcely be described as a non-event. There was a 'mole' within the Nationwide, and a 'secret memo' from a general manager was leaked a few days before the AGM. The memo recommended that 'members of staff from all parts of the United Kingdom' should be encouraged to give 'maximum support' to the Chairman and Chief General Manager, while making scrupulously clear that all travel, subsistence entertainment or accommodation charges would have to be borne by the individuals concerned. Since 'attention is entirely a matter of personal choice' it was suggested that staff should dress informally (wives or friends too!) and should not display the membership badges of Rotary, Round Table or Lion as these 'might point to the presence at the meeting of a group of members of staff'. Should there be a 'demand' from 'other members of the society' for information about the number of members of staff present, such members were advised to 'ignore any such request' unless the Chairman advised otherwise. Indeed it was hoped that in any event staff members would subsequently make it clear to the meeting that they were attending in a private capacity. Staff members were further advised that the meeting was 'likely to be protracted' and they should be prepared to be present throughout the proceedings, however long these might run. The memo went on to suggest that consideration be given to 'planting' some members of staff to ask questions that the directors would wish to hear. Finally it warned staff to take care of what and where they spoke: 'staircases, the foyer, toilets, or even outside the building. It should be remembered that it would be quite possible for Mr Punt or one of his supporters to be standing within a yard or two of such a group and a conversation could easily be heard and a remark used later in another context.'

Hamish McRae, financial editor of *The Guardian*, expresses the feelings of many on hearing of this document.

Now the sort of tactics that are proposed would be perfectly familiar to extreme political groups eager to use an apparently democratic forum to endorse its views. But this is not an extreme political group. It is the top management of one of the largest building societies in the land. Above it sits a board of distinguished and wholly honourable men.

Could they really support a plan that borrows the tactics of extreme political organisations which they would surely be the first to condemn?[4]

Perhaps because of this, 1,000 Nationwide members turned up at the AGM the following day to hear the directors variously likened to King Canute and aristocrats, and described as 'undemocratic and autocratic' in their opposition to change.[5]

Analysis of the case

Punt v Nationwide may be analyzed from many different aspects. It may be seen, like any other dispute, as a collection of disagreements and misunderstandings concerning the assumptions and meanings contained within a set of propositions. Such an analysis could well be useful, as a major controversy centres on what is 'in the interests of members'. Clearly, Punt and the board of directors are in complete disagreement — not least because there is little guidance about what such pious words actually mean.

Although we have looked at the conflict as an economic one, it can also be regarded from a social standpoint. On one hand are the old upper classes, and on the other are the new working classes. One is reminded of the report in *The Guardian* on the 1982 AGM.

'The sociologists have found a new victim' remarked one director gloomily. 'Look at those bearded chaps in their sweaters and trousers. They are all at Kingston Poly, and good luck to them. But they are not our kind of saver.'[6]

The 'bearded chaps' are spurred on by the encouraging publicity of *The Guardian*.

The case can rightly be seen as a modern class conflict. This book has attempted to show how building societies, in a subtle way, are a major mechanism for helping the rich get richer and depriving the poor.

It also shows how quickly the original issues are obscured by the tactics, strategies and arms of war. It is not clear from the resolutions, the changed proxy forms and other paraphernalia what all the fuss is about. But it is wrong to suppose that the issues are forgotten, or go unnoticed. This case, as much as anything, caused Sir Geoffrey Howe on 18 May 1982 to promise new legislation regarding building societies during the next parliament; a major issue to be settled would be the conduct of meetings and the respective rights and duties of members and directors. On the other hand, Punt has so embittered the existing Nationwide directors that any proposals he may make within the democratic framework of that society will no doubt be resisted all the way.

The regulation of limited companies

Problems concerning the management and conduct of limited companies are resolved to a large extent through the operation of the market system. Many of the problems that are comparable to those outlined in the earlier chapters of this book are handled by shareholders by selling their shares, and even by the company going out of business. But this cannot happen with building societies — members can only go to another society, which probably offers very similar terms. There are further mechanisms for companies. In the case of the larger ones and where there are large institutional shareholdings such as pension funds, various 'voluntary' arrangements exist. The Wilson Committee write:

> In general, a substantial community of interest between institutional and other shareholders does doubtless exist. It is in everybody's interest that weak or inadequate management should be challenged and that efficient management should not be allowed to rest on its laurels. In undertaking this function the institutions will normally be acting in a way which is of advantage to all shareholders.[7]

They cite the collective action of the institutions through the Investment Protection Committees and the Institutional Shareholders Committee although they acknowledge that 'Many of those giving evidence to us were extremely sceptical about the scope of what could be done.'[8] The most concerted action by institutional shareholders is probably when they sell out of a company or force a complete management or financial re-organisation.

But there are stringent 'voluntary' arrangements especially

concerning the rights of shareholders and the conduct and duties of directors, notably in connection with takeovers and mergers. The Stock Exchange 'code of conduct' is considered good and acceptable practice. Non-compliance with this code may bring expulsion from the city, for example in suspension of share-price and blacking by brokers. There are many other voluntary, semi-voluntary and legal regulations governing the conduct of companies and their directors, mainly in their share dealings and the Stock Exchange. The objective of all these regulations is to ensure a fair and proper market in the shares of the company; it is assumed that this can only come about if shareholders are fairly treated. Often this is achieved by the provision of all the information necessary to make a decision.

Of course, not everything can be resolved in this way. The law recognizes this and gives the Department of Trade and Industry major investigatory powers, compulsory winding up of the company and the takeover of the management of the company by the official receiver or another official appointed by the shareholders. Perhaps of more importance is the assumption in the philosophy of company law that shareholders, or any group of them, may be oppressed by the directors and/or other shareholders. For example, Section 210 of the 1948 Companies Act ensures that any member who complains that the affairs of the company are being conducted in a manner oppressive to some of the members, including the complainer, may petition the court for an order under that section. Again, Section 5 enables dissident holders of 15 per cent of the issued shares to apply to the court for the cancellation of an alteration of the objects of the company (which determine what type of business it does).

There is also the assumption that customers and suppliers need protecting from the company, not least because it has 'limited liability'. There are provisions against the directors and shareholders 'milking' the company and leaving it with no funds for creditors. Provisions also exist for the inspection of company accounts and registers and incorporation documents either at the company's registered office or at Companies Registration Office.

Great effort has gone into ensuring the fair and efficient running of limited companies: a particular concern of the Department of

Trade and Industry. The concept of a limited company is ingenious; most of industry and commerce is run in such a way that companies receive long-term capital whilst investors lend short-term (they may sell their shares).

Final remarks

The case of Punt v Nationwide is not unique. That of Twyman v the Anglia is remarkably similar, the same issues were at stake, it was fought in a similar way, and therefore has not been reported here. That Twyman eventually became a director is perhaps a chance occurrence. Perhaps, as Twyman himself believes, he had 'earned their grudging respect for my activities; they also had the opportunity to check more closely into background and experience — hence their decision to invite me on to the Board, so that the new society would benefit from my energy, qualifications and experience'.[9] Or perhaps to go through another major merger (with the London & South of England) and face Twyman's able opposition was unpalatable; possibly it was deemed sensible to take him on board. The alternative could have been to reject the merger, in which case Twyman would have continued his campaign, presumably until he tired of the whole affair. Both cases suggest that the immense inadequacies of the system cannot simply be left to Mr Punt and his relatively small band of followers in the Building Societies Members Association to remedy.

For many reasons, there may be consumer dissatisfaction with a society. But there are few mechanisms for the resolution of such disputes other than the members' meeting. On the other hand, in the case of the limited company, there are many sophisticated mechanisms to resolve shareholder dissatisfaction and conflict. And traders can always go to another company. Building societies are in a monopolistic position: they can outprice competitors mainly because of the tax benefits and, as it is, they all offer very similar terms.

Either the concept of a building society has to be recognized as an ingenious idea — with savers lending short, borrowers borrowing long and thereby providing great benefits to house buyers — or this virtue has been forgotten, and the necessary mechanisms for its preservation have not been put into effect. We consider the action of the Registrar of Friendly Societies in more detail later; earlier chapters and the case study all suggest that the powers and duties of the chief registrar are very restricted. For example, when a member is in dispute with his society, it can be resolved if they complete the necessary forms. On the other hand, if they disagree about this, the procedure breaks down and the Registry's power of resolution is rendered ineffective.

The case study indicates that there is a case for reform. When it comes to the crunch, the member is powerless, and may even be expelled, irrespective of how genuine the grievances, and important the questions are. When, as the Annual Return shows, a Nationwide director has an outstanding mortgage of £34,650 at an interest rate of 5 per cent when the BSA recommended rate is 10 per cent (31 December 1982), members are entitled to question whether such rules should be part of the way the society is run.

The major point is that the simple resolution of conflict through members meetings and through adjudications and so on by the chief registrar is inadequate — especially when compared with company law, for instance, which is based on more realistic assumptions. Building society law would seem not to recognize the possibility of conflict and disputes — indeed it *assumes* mutuality.

12. Proposals for reform

The need for reform lies in the revelation of an important difference between what exists and what may have been commonly thought to, or 'should' exist. That there is a difference between 'acceptable' and 'good' practice, and actuality, is recognized by the new Chief Registrar of Friendly Societies. His 1981/82 annual report demonstrates this most clearly on such matters as the expulsion of a member (the Paddington episode, see page 67), the declaration of interests by staff and others at meetings, and the elections of directors.[1] However the upholding of the spirit of the law by the chief registrar in other than an *ex poste* way has yet to be seen.

But what needs reforming and how? In this chapter we shall compare the objectives of building societies with practice, thereby identifying some areas for reform. In the light of the promised new Building Societies Act we shall then discuss how these reforms may be achieved and what succeful legislation can be made.

The objectives of building societies

The law on objectives is quite clear (see chapter 2), but we need to go further. The aim of building societies is to raise money to promote home ownership. As building societies are the main source of housing finance, they are required to raise an amount which enables as many people as possible to own their own homes.

Do we need building societies to do this job? Couldn't the high street banks easily take over the role? If the answer is 'yes', we should expect something further from building societies than what is provided by the banks. I am talking here not only of their efficiency, but more importantly of their efficacy. We would expect building societies not only to raise sufficient funds, but also to distribute them amongst those most in need of mortgages. Building societies have a responsibility to the total quality of housing *in addition to* the basic business and prudential criteria. In other words, we would expect them to develop some considerable expertise in the housing market as a concomitant to their responsibility for the housing needs of the total community.

Finally, it is now accepted that tax concessions and subsidies should be supplied to help with the provision of housing and for building societies to achieve these objectives. We would expect these benefits to be used accordingly.

How well do building societies achieve these objectives? Not well, it seems, although it is difficult to assess to what extent, and to evaluate all the aspects and implications. Building societies borrow proportionately more from the lower income groups and lend proportionally more to higher ones. The cartel causes mortgage shortages and not all funds go for home loans, and certainly not to the most needy. Mortgages are decided mainly on commercial criteria and the societies are managed as businesses; monopolistic positions are created and exploited, although the non-profit objective perverts managerial motives and decisions. Building societies do not usually go beyond these business and prudential aspects; neither does the Registrar of Friendly Societies.

Attempts to reform: breaking the cartel

Almost the only acceptance of the need for reform coming from within the movement has been by Abbey National Building Society and its chief executive, Clive Thornton. In recent years the Abbey National has broken away from, or led, other societies on many issues. It has attempted to establish its activities in Europe, it has pioneered the presentation of valuers' reports to house buyers, it has worked towards change in the provision of both housing finance in inner-city areas. More recently it has attempted to break the formal BSA cartel arrangement, regarding which, Clive Thornton's comments on *The Money Programme* in October 1983 (and subsequent events) are most poignant. To quote, on the voluntary nature of the recommended rate system whereby the large societies are forced to 'toe the line' and the small not so:

Thornton   Why should an investor of the Halifax get less than an investor of the London Permanent and the Greenwich? They are all members of the same association, all voted for the same structure [of interest rates] and so the Halifax members are being short-changed, and that is what we are on about. . . . We [Abbey National] have had enough of that sort of thing.

Widlake   Is the cartel finished?

Thornton   It's dead now.

Widlake   You've been accused of being ungentlemanly. Do you think you have been?

Thornton   If ever you rock the boat in any trade association or profession that doesn't like change, then it's ungentlemanly. But then perhaps I've never been a gentleman.

Within a few days it was announced that Clive Thornton was to leave Abbey National to become executive chair of the Mirror Group of Newspapers. It may be wrong to interpret this as expulsion due to ungentlemanly conduct, since within a few days the BSA recommended rate system was formally cancelled. It was replaced by a system whereby the BSA 'advises' on rates, leaving members free to set their own. The 28-day rule (societies had to give 28 days' notice of changes of rates not covered by the cartel) was also replaced by an agreement that societies would talk to the BSA about their plans and 'give adequate notice of their intentions'. To help consultation, the BSA would set up a system for societies to swap information about interest rates.[2]

Does this represent any real change? The new arrangements sound very like the old ones. Thornton's interview and subsequent developments may provide an insight. His reasons for the abandonment of the cartel were quite technical. They involved the injustice of the arrangement whereby the interest rate offered by the large society on ordinary shares was less than that offered by smaller societies for ordinary shares. Large societies were forced to abide by these arrangements, but smaller societies (because of their economic insignificance) were not. (See chapters 3, 4 and 7.)

This suited many large societies anyway as it enabled them to offer high-interest term shares. Ordinary share rates were used to subsidize term share rates. So the recommended rate system itself had very little influence on the funds collected, and the rates charged and paid, by both individual societies and the movement. And differential mortgage rates were introduced as and when societies felt it necessary. The simple point is this: the change from one effectively voluntary system to another voluntary system is unlikely to have any real effect. The basic financing structure and terms (ordinary shares and deposits, term shares etc.) are determined by the individual society and the overall interest rates are in any case determined from outside.

What may be expected, and would be widely applauded, is for building society interest rates to become less rigid, changing more frequently with interest rates generally. The policy of stabilization was cited (see chapter 4) as the worst effect of the recommended rate, causing feast and famine in the mortgage markets, which in turn led to boom and depression in the house building industry, and probably beyond. If this is the effect, it is indeed a reform. However, the evidence is that the stabilized interest rate policy has remained. Nothing has changed.

Has the cartel really been broken? An attempt was made by one society, perhaps even one man, who has since left the society. Chapter 4 argues that it is not possible for one firm alone to break an oligopoly. Price wars do occur from time to time in oligopolistic industries, but they result in huge losses and financial crashes. There can be no possibility of this in the building society industry. Members fix a cartel arrangement that is mutually acceptable, and it matters little whether it is formal or agreed behind closed doors. The BSA cartel has been mutually acceptable not least because it allows complete flexibility. All societies have been able to use it as they wish. From time to time other large societies have opted out of the cartel for short periods, only to come back again later. The Halifax did so a few years ago. The Abbey has stated its inability to go it alone this time.

But there has been an effect. Formal abandonment of the cartel is particularly convenient now, when there is so much criticism of the movement and when the law is about to be changed. Much of this criticism focuses on the effects of the recommended rate system; with the abandonment of the cartel much of the consumer-lobby case would collapse.

The required reforms are more profound; abolition of the recommended rate system may be a red herring. There is no indication that it will be replaced by a set of arrangements which are in any way different. There is certainly no evidence that the inevitability of cartel arrangements in all oligopolies has somehow ceased to apply to building societies. For these reasons the cartel will continue until the monopoly is broken.

Reforms through taxation

The building societies' monopoly power has developed through their domination of the housing and personal savings markets and the emergence of big countrywide societies. The reason for the former is that the building societies enjoy a privileged competitive position due to their taxation treatment. If this were removed — particularly the composite-rate arrangement which leads to important inequities amongst savers (non-taxpayers subsidizing taxpayers) — then the building societies' competitive advantage would be cut at a stroke.

But can the subsidization of housing still be achieved? Yes, and easily, if all tax concessions are provided to mortgagors rather than to both the building societies and mortgagors. The present arrangements (described in chapter 3) provide tax benefits to the building societies on their inflow and processing of funds (the composite rate and reduced corporation tax rates respectively). These should be removed and the full taxation subsidy provided to the mortgagor. Taxation benefits should also be progressive, the needy receiving larger proportions; the present regressive arrangements give the very low income groups few benefits. One suggestion is that taxation benefits need not be related to the interest-paid portion but instead to the total payment (principal plus interest) repaid during the year and the income of the tax payer. Such a system has further attributes. The building societies would only be able to attract the same amount of funds through efficiency of operations and passing back mortgagors' tax benefits to savers through the interest rates offered. This could only be achieved by making full use of a differential rate structure on mortgages related to the size and risk of the mortgage, and preferring mortgagors with the relatively larger tax benefits: those most in need of mortgages.

Reform: managerial standards

But not all reforms can be achieved by taxation change. Major reform is required in the quality, duties and rights of society management. The iniquities outlined earlier were attributed to the objectives and motivations of building society directors. There are suggestions of other managerial inadequacies. One large society, the Britannia, even failed to present a correct, audited, annual return at the second attempt.[3]

The absence of the profit motive, and the restrictions laid down by the 1962 Act on the type of business conducted, affects the kind of person likely to work for a building society. If entrepreneurial and business talent is not rewarded, it will not be attracted. There are other effects. It's an easy life in a building society. Those looking for a soft option join and are protected; the more confident go elsewhere. Of building society chiefs, Graham Turner recently wrote: 'As a breed they are courteous, rather colourless souls who have the aspect of municipal treasurers rather than entrepreneurs though they are often paid more like the latter', and, further, that Clive Thornton 'believes that the charge of sterility is amply justified; that building societies should have grown into a £75 billion industry and done nothing about housing policy is, he says, dreadful'.[4]

The dearth of talent on the boards of many building societies, and managerial standards need not be accepted. *The Economist* recently took this up in general terms in a discussion of the proposal of the original Spalding Report that building societies should move into other kinds of business, such as estate agency and banking:

As quasi-bankers, they will have to judge a customer's credit-worthiness on grounds other than the normally rock-solid collateral of housing. Nothing in the way building societies are run at present, or in the background of the men who administer them, yet suggests that they are up to the tasks ahead.[5]

The main justification for these assertions is the age and occupations of directors. Often they have very limited experience of the business world outside building societies, and only very local knowledge and experience. The average age of building society directors is shocking: at the end of 1982 it was 65 at the Nationwide, 64 at the Alliance and the Bradford and Bingley, 67 at the Gateway, and 69 at the Britannia.

Perhaps this is the final dilemma, that many building societies are 'self-perpetuating oligarchies' and that legislation alone cannot cure the malaise. 'It helps to be old, it helps to be local and it helps to be related to other members of the board.'[6]

The men at the top — the boards of directors — determine the standards and conduct of those below them. They are responsible. The official reports on the Grays and the Alfreton scandals expressed concern over the calibre, age and experience of building society directors; the findings suggested that in many societies standards of financial control may not be sufficiently high. This has been the subject of constant anxiety for the Registry of Friendly Society staff.

- Between January 1980 and June 1982 the Registry made 130 inspection visits.
- The Chief Registrar wrote to chairs of all societies in January and August 1981, reminding them of their statutory obligations and exhorting them to attend a seminar on director responsibilities and financial control.
- Registry staff have contributed 'significantly' to seminars arranged by the accountancy profession on financial control.
- The Chief Registrar made a stern statement on the duty of directors in the section on small societies in the 1981/82 annual report.

But financial control is the bare essential. Building society directors are charged with a responsibility to housing policy and conditions, about which they have done very little. What is needed desperately is fewer directors with vested interests in the society's business, and more with industrial experience and, more importantly, *people who represent housing needs*.

The experiences of Twyman at the Anglia and Punt at the Nationwide are significant. While they demonstrate the intransigence of the existing boards they also demonstrate a recognition by society at large that there is a need for change. Twyman's success, however paradoxical, demonstrated how conflict brings about change. That is likely to continue. While boards of directors, faced by genuine questions by members, respond by writing silly secret memos to staff asking them to infiltrate members meetings, expelling members, suing them, or revealing how much they have in their accounts, they will be scorned and humiliated by the media. When the all-expenses-paid BSA trip to Australia, including 'a race afternoon, orientation tour of Melbourne, cocktail reception' hits the *Daily Mirror* Paul Foot column[7], as a sarcastic explanation of why the ordinary person cannot get a mortgage, then the building societies are truly facing widespread criticism.

Reform: the role of members and directors

A prerequisite of a more responsible building society movement is recognition of the role of members — that they require information and power to create more effective societies — similar to a prerequisite for any democratic organization, including even the limited company.

The usual view of those within the building society movement is that members are just customers, and that their rights should be curtailed. The Spalding Report[8] proposed restricting the powers of members further and providing them with much less information. Similar views are expressed by other so-called research reports.[9]

The present arrangements for member rights are both inefficient and ineffective. The voting system is ridiculous, whilst proxy systems are such that directors can easily block proposals by large numbers of members, as in the Nationwide and Anglia cases. Voting should be made much easier for members. It need not, and should not, involve complicated forms that must be posted to a head office. If the issues were explained to members, who could cast votes at a convenient branch, then some sense would be imported into the proceedings.

The forthcoming Building Societies Act, therefore, needs to clarify and ensure the rights and role of members. At the moment the law is so equivocal that a leading export on building society law could stand up at a members meeting and argue, on the directors' behalf, that the members had no rights regarding the policy of their society.[10] Such uncertainty, if it exists, must surely be removed.

The important reform, however, concerns information. The annual return contains much data that is largely irrelevant and meaningless to ordinary investors. It was designed not for them, but for the Registry of Friendly Societies' prudential purposes. It is clear from chapter 7 that a definition and concept of profit concerning investment gains needs to be agreed. The current format of the annual accounts may be sufficient for the prudential purposes of a member. More important is information about the society's lending policy, the likelihood of a member getting a mortgage, and facts about the society's 'housing policy'. At present these are conspicuously absent and entirely preclude any debate on the policies and practices of a society. Until such a time as members and the public are aware of the implications of building society behaviour on housing, there will be indifference, and no check and debate on policy. In the meantime many small societies, valuable for their housing policies, may continue to be absorbed by merger without the important issues ever being considered. Invariably members are given little useful information about merger proposals. For example, we are still at a loss to know completely why the announced merger proposals between the Town and Country and the Midshires, and between the Chelsea and the Coventry Economic, were abandoned. The brief public statements simply discussed non-compatibility, but such matters are usually resolved at a very early stage before any announcement of intended merger.

Members, and society at large, require relevant information concerning building society policies and proposals. The forthcoming act should legislate for this.

Important legislation is required concerning the duties and obligations of directors. Firstly, the disclosure of their interests is insufficient. Section 73 of the 1962 Act requires a director to declare to the other directors any interest he might have in a contract with the society. This does not have to be in writing, nor disclosed to either the members or the Registrar of Friendly Societies — far too sloppy a practice. It is suggested here that building society law should at least be brought in line with company law, which requires further disclosure. Secondly, the requirements concerning advances to directors are inadequate. At present loans to directors, their nominees, and their companies are only required to be disclosed in the society's annual returns. The provisions need extending to include loans to close family members.

A fair proportion of this book has been devoted to special advances to companies. While the BSA accepts that such loans are undesirable, the Spalding Report has recommended that they should not be identified as a separate class of loans and that there need be no information reported concerning them. Clearly this would be unacceptable as it is a reversion to the pre 1960 situation whereby some societies lent vast sums to directors' and their associates' companies. It is suggested here that all loans to companies (other than for building finance, which should be regulated) should be legislated against. It is sometimes argued that granting special advances is justified at times of slack mortgage demand. However there is little evidence to suggest that, overall, the proportion of new funds in special advance decreases in periods of excessive mortgage demand, and increases in slack periods.[11]

The failure of the New Cross more than any other event has demonstrated the need for reform of the law and the way in which it is policed. The regulations, as they stand, go nowhere near to dealing with the causes of a financial collapse. The reasons for the New Cross downfall involved an over-ambitious chair and imprudent financing. The regulations conspicuously ignore these factors. Even so the ratios were exceeded and ignored. The New Cross is not the only case. The Registry of Friendly Societies needs further powers; it also needs higher skills in order to judge when to act.

The above provisions are necessary in order to establish a new context in which building societies are managed. If societies are to be concerned with the wider social aspects of housing, the business advantages to directors need to be constrained. If reform is to come it must be led by a wider breadth of directors who are not solely concerned with business interests.

Change

In the last two decades, the small mutual building society has been replaced by huge multi-billion pound societies with countrywide networks. These operate as monopolistic businesses that have neglected their responsibilities to provide home ownership for all, and particularly the poorer classes. This is unacceptable: if building societies are to operate in this way they might as well be banks or become parts of banks, without all the privileges afforded the societies.

The new Building Societies Act should legislate reform in taxation, the rights and role of members, the duties of directors, the provision of useful and necessary information to evaluate the effectiveness and responsiveness to societies. The building societies have had plenty of time to put their houses in order and yet they have demonstrated no desire to do so. The so-called abolition of the cartel was nothing more then a publicity exercise to divert criticism on the eve of the new act.

At the time of writing it still is not certain whether the new Building Societies Act will include the wide-ranging reforms suggested here. If it does not it will be a pity: housing standards for the poor are the worst for a long time. The building societies should be able to help the country's housing problems. More responsible and responsive societies are urgently needed.

Appendix. The Wakefield Letter

REGISTRY OF FRIENDLY SOCIETIES
17 North Audley Street London W1Y 2AP

Telephone 01-629 7001 ext

Please reply to The Registrar
Your reference

Our reference

Date   16 September 1976

Dear Sir

Although defalcations of any size by building society employees are relatively rare, instances have recently come to my notice in which the sums were misappropriated over periods of years without detection. I have no doubt that directors of building societies are fully conscious of their general duty to safeguard a society's funds. It seems to me appropriate however to draw your Board's attention to the particular duties expressly imposed upon a society and on its directors by section 76 of the Building Societies Act 1962 and in particular section 76(1)(b).

Under section 76(1)(b) it is the duty of a society to establish and maintain –

(1) a system of control and inspection of its books of account, and

(2) a system for supervising its cash holdings and all remittances and receipts.

By virtue of section 76(5) directors are required to take all reasonable steps to ensure that a society has established and maintains these systems.

The establishment and maintenance of these systems is intended to prevent, so far as is practicably possible, misappropriations and other misuses of a society's funds. Whilst I appreciate that it may be impossible to prevent all misappropriations, the systems mentioned should be such that if unfortunately money is misappropriated the matter will be brought to light within a short time.

I do not think it is practical for me to suggest the lines on which these systems should operate as so much depends on a society's size and number of staff. It is for directors to satisfy themselves that whatever systems they maintain are effective to disclose irregularities, whether in books of account or the handling of cash and cheques and by whomsoever committed. No one handling books or cash should escape this system, however senior or trusted he may be.

Directors will have noted that auditors are required under section 87(4) of the Act to consider, amongst other matters, whether a society has maintained a satisfactory system of control so as to comply with s.76(1)(b) and to report if in their opinion it has not. In this connexion I ought to emphasise that directors should not consider that s.76(1)(b) has been complied with merely because the auditors have not reported to the contrary. It is the director's responsibility and not the auditor's to ensure that compliance is effective.

I am writing in similar terms to all Chairmen of societies and would ask you to bring this letter to the attention of the Board when it next meets. In the course of the next few months I will be approaching a number of societies for information about how they are meeting the requirements of the Building Societies Act 1962 in the matter of control.

Yours faithfully

Notes

1. Official and consumer criticism

1. National Board for Prices and Incomes, *Rates of Interest on Building Society Mortgages, Report No. 22, Cmnd 3136, HMSO 1966.*
2. Committee to review the Functioning of Financial Institutions, *Report* (The Wilson Report), Cmnd. 7937, HMSO 1980.
3. National Consumer Council, *Building Societies and the Consumer*, A Report by M. Rigg and M. Young of the Mutual Aid Centre, 1981.
4. S. Weir, 'Red line districts', *Roof*, July 1976, p. 109-14.
5. 'Estate agents "discriminate against coloured applicants" ', *Building Societies Gazette*, October 1980, p. 1300.
6. A report by the Consumer Association Survey Unit for the Equal Opportunities Commission, *It's Not Your Business, It's How the Society Works*, August 1978, and quoted in National Consumer Council report, op. cit.
7. 'The houses women buy', *Evening Standard*, 6 February 1979.
8. J. Tunnard, 'The mortgage rows', *Roof*, 1978.
9. National Consumer Council, op. cit.
10. National Consumer Council, op. cit.

2. How the societies are run

1. E. Gauldie, *Cruel Habitations: A History of Working Class Housing, 1780-1918*, Allen & Unwin 1974.
2. *First Report of the Commissioners appointed to enquire into Friendly and Benefit Societies, with minutes of evidence*, HMSO 1871.
3. *Evidence submitted by the Building Societies Association to the Committee to Review the Functioning of Financial Institutions*, BSA 1978.
4. E.A. Wurtzburg and J. Mills, *Building Society Law*, Stevens 1976.
5. *Report of the Chief Registrar of Friendly Societies* Part 2, Building Societies, 1978 Appendix, pp. 38, 39.

6. ibid.
7. Wurtzburg and Mills, op. cit. p. 330.
8. *The Sunday Times*, 'Mortgage mischief', 24 January 1982.
9. Letter to *Accountancy*, October 1980, p. 36.

3. Building society operations

1. P. Court, 'Too many whales and minnows', *Accountancy Age*, 11 August 1978, pp. 7–8.
2. Committee to Review the Functioning of Financial Institutions, *Report* (the Wilson Report), Cmnd. 7937, HMSO 1980, para. 245.
3. For example see the Wilson Report, op.cit.; and National Consumer Council, *Building Societies and the Consumer*, A Report by M. Rigg and M. Young of the Mutual Aid Centre, 1981.
4. M. Boddy, *The Building Societies*, Macmillan 1980, p. 63.
5. ibid., p. 65.
6. This is axiomatic; but see also M. Boddy, op. cit., pp. 58–9.
7. Department of Environment circular 24/66.
8. *Housing Policy: A Consultative Document*, Technical Volume Part 2, Cmnd. 6851/HMSO 1977, p. 154 note 13.
9. Rule Five, the Ecology Building Society.
10. *Report of the Chief Registrar of Friendly Societies, 1977* Part 2, Building Societies.
11. Wilson Report, op. cit., para 700.
12. ibid., para 692.
13. J. Foster, 'The redistributive effect of inflation on building society shares and deposits 1961-74', *Bulletin of Economic Research*, November 1976, pp. 67–76.
14. Wilson Report, *op. cit.,* para 698.

4. Building society economics

1. P. Barnes, 'Break up the building societies' cartel — yes but how?', *Accountancy*, August 1980, p. 56.
2. E.H. Chamberlain, *The Theory of Monopolistic Competition*, Cambridge, Mass.: Harvard University Press 1933, 6th edition, p. 48.
3. F.M. Scherer, *Industrial Market Structure and Economic Performance*, Chicago: Rand McNally College Publishing 1980, 2nd edition, p. 155.
4. B. Lowes and J.R. Sparks, *Modern Managerial Economics*, Heinemann 1974, p. 188.
5. Quoted in Scherer op. cit., p. 16.
6. Committee to Review the Functioning of Financial Institutions,

Report (the Wilson Report), Cmnd. 7937, HMSO 1980, para 388.

7. Scherer op cit. p. 317

8. P. Doyle and G.D. Newbould, 'Marketing strategies for building societies', *Management Decision*, vol. 13 no.1, 1975, pp. 41–50.

9. R.L. Harrington, 'Housing — supply and demand', *National Westminster Bank Review*, May 1972, p. 48.

10. For further evidence and discussion of these matters see T.J. Gough, *Housing Policy and the Distribution of Income and Wealth in the UK*, UWIST Discussion Paper in Economics, Finance and Politics, no. 1, May 1976; and J. Foster, 'The redistributive effect of inflation on building society shares and deposits, 1961–74, *Bulletin of Economic Research*, November 1976, pp. 67–76.

11. T.J. Gough, 'Phases of British private housebuilding and the supply of mortgage credit', *Applied Economics*, September 1975, pp. 213–22.

12. ibid.

5. Manager's non-accountability

1. For example Monsen and others tested the hypothesis that owner-controlled firms were more profitable than manager-controlled firms. The results revealed that the former outperformed the latter 'by a considerable margin' and that the size effect (the latter would tend to be larger firms) was insignificant. R.J. Monsen, J.S. Chiv and D.E. Cooley, 'The effects of separation of ownership and control on the performance of the large firm' *Quarterly Journal of Economics* August 1968, pp. 435–51.

2. C. Kaysen, 'The corporation: how much power? what scope?' in E.S. Mason (ed.), *The Corporation in Modern Society*, Cambridge 1960.

3. R.A. Gordon, *Business Leadership in the Large Corporation*, Berkeley, 1961.

4. O.E. Williamson, 'Managerial discretion and business behaviour', *American Economic Review*, December 1963, p. 1032–57.

5. ibid.

6. ibid.

7. See for example H. Leibenstein, *Beyond Economic Man: A New Foundation for Microeconomics*, Cambridge, Mass.: Harvard University Press 1976.

8. J.A. Verbrugge, J.E. Hillard and H.M. Davis, 'X-inefficiency, market structure and form of organisation: evidence from the financial sector', *Industrial Organisational Review*, vol. 6 no. 1, 1978, pp. 29–37.

9. It was hypothesized that, as the concentration of SLAs in a particular

US state increased, the likelihood of aggressive competition decreased. Since price competition between financial institutions may be limited, non-price aspects, such as loan output, were also considered. H.M. Davis and J.A. Verbrugge, 'Structure and performance in the savings and loan industry', *Journal of Economics and Business*. Fall 1978, pp. 40–51.

10. Mortgage yields and fee income were most noticeably related to profits. J.A. Verbrugge and R.A. Shick, 'Market structure and savings and loan profitability', *Quarterly Review of Economics and Business*, Summer 1976, pp. 79–96.

11. For details, of this and other tests described in this section, see P.A. Barnes, 'Financial performance of UK building societies during the 1970s — managerial motives and constraints', unpublished Ph.D. thesis, University of Sheffield, 1982. Copies of the relevant chapters may be obtained from the author.

12. ibid.

13. G. Davies and M.J. Davies, *Building Societies and their branches: A Regional Economic Survey*, Franey & Co. 1981, pp.172–3.

14. See P. A Barnes, op. cit.

15. Davies and Davies, op. cit.

16. P. A. Barnes and J.C. Dodds, 'The structure and performance of the UK building society industry 1970–78', *Journal of Business Finance and Accounting*, Spring 1983, pp. 37–56.

17. ibid.

6. Growth through merger

1. *Report of the Chief Registrar of Friendly Societies for the year 1970*, Part 2: Building Societies, HMSO.

2. *Report of the Chief Registrar of Friendly Societies*, 1980, HMSO.

3. P. Court, 'Too many whales and minnows', *Accountancy Age*, 11 August 1978, pp. 7–8.

4. G. Meeks, *Disappointing Marriage: A Study of the Gains from Mergers*, Cambridge University Press 1977, p. 10.

5. J.C.B. Cooper, 'Economies of scale in the UK building society industry', *Investment Analyst*, January 1980, pp. 31–7.

6. T.J. Gough, 'Building society mergers and the size-efficiency relationship', *Applied Economics*, June 1979, pp. 185–94.

7. D. Gilchrist and S. Rothwell, 'Mergers of medium societies should mean more efficiency', *Building Societies Gazette*, January 1980, pp. 20–22.

8. P.A. Barnes and J.C. Dodds, 'Building society mergers and the

size-efficiency relationship — a comment', *Applied Economics*, December 1981, pp. 531–4.

9. These are not presented here for reasons of space. See P.A. Barnes, 'The financial performance of UK building societies during the 1970s — managerial motives and constraints', unpublished Ph.D. thesis, University of Sheffield, 1982. Copies of the relevant chapter may be obtained directly from the author. Note that the statistics were appropriately weighted for relative size of merging societies and tested for statistical significance.

10. ibid.

11. This is cleary opposite to what may be expected by conventional economic theory assuming profit maximization. In the long term, minimum unit cost firms would emerge through mergers etc. See for example G.J. Stigler, 'The economies of scale', *Journal of Law and Economics*, January 1958, pp. 54–71; and R.D. Rees, 'Optimum plant size in United Kingdom industries: some survivor estimates', *Economica*, November 1973, pp. 394–401.

12. P. Court, op. cit.

13. 'Members should have more information on merger proposals — chief registrar', *Building Societies Gazette*, June 1982, p. 658.

14. 'Accrington transfer follows biggest hearing for 10 years', *Building Societies Gazette*, August 1982, pp. 1039–40.

15. ibid.

16. ibid.

17. E. Clouston, 'One pound one vote', *The Guardian*, 19 March 1983, p. 7.

18. *Report of the Chief Registrar 1981-1982*, p. 18.

19. Quoted in 'Chief registrar confirms Goldhawk payment to auditors', *Building Societies Gazette*, June 1980, p. 650.

20. *Report of the Chief Registrar of Friendly Societies for the year 1968*, Part 2, Building Societies, p. 39.

21. ibid. p. 42.

22. ibid.

23. ibid. p. 47.

24. ibid. p. 48

7. Accounting practices

1. *Guide to Building Society Finance*, BSA, 2nd edition, 1980, para. 1.23.

2. op. cit., para. 1.22.

3. *Building Societies Gazette*, December 1980, p. 1608.

4. Tony Levene, 'Gilts Upset for State Borrowing', *Sunday Times*, 26 February 1984.

5. op. cit,. para 3.58, 3.59.

6. P.A. Barnes, 'Are building societies overcompeting?', *Accountancy*, October 1981, pp.130–132.

7. L. Williams, *Building Society Accounts*, 3rd edn, The Building Societies Institute 1978, p.87.

8. The BSA requires that every member should have reserves in excess of those required for trustee investment as defined in the Building Societies (Designation for Trustee Investment) Regulations, 1972. These are that a society's reserves must be not less than $2\frac{1}{2}$ per cent of its assets not exceeding £100 million, 2 per cent of its assets exceeding £100 million, but not exceeding £500 million, and 1.25 per cent of its assets exceeding £1,000 million. If a society is growing, the difficulties in maintaining the reserve ratio are increased.

9. For a full description of the research study see 'The consequence of growth maximisation and expense preference policies of managers: evidence from the UK Building Societies. A study of the causes of profit insufficiency during a period of increased competition using discriminant analysis', *Journal of Business Finance and Accounting*, Winter 1983, pp.521–30. Discriminant analysis estimates weights attributable to the variables . These weights are not reported here as their interpretation must be made in the terms of the statistical technique used.

10. See, for example, Peter Shearlock, 'Gilt groans', *Sunday Times*, 4 March 1984.

8. 'Managerial diversion'

1. A. Tech, *Mutual Savings Banks and Savings and Loan Associations*, New York: Columbia University Press 1968, p. 38.

2. A. Nichols, *Management and Control in the Mutual Savings and Loan Associations*, Lexington, Mass.: Lexington Books 1972, chapter 1.

3. ibid., chapter 15.

4. E.J. Cleary, *The Building Society Movement*, Elek 1965, chapters 13 and 14.

5. *Report of the Chief Registrar of Friendly Societies for the year 1954*, Part 5. Building Societies, p. 5.

6. *Report of the Chief Registrar of Friendly Societies for the year 1959*, p. 15.

7. ibid.

8. *Board of Trade Inspectors Report*, H. Jasper & Co. Ltd., 1959.
9. *Report of the Chief Registrar of Friendly Societies for the year 1960*, Appendix III, Report of the Inspector appointed to examine into the Affairs of the State B.S.
10. O. Marriott, *The Property Boom*, Pan Piper 1967, pp. 108–9.
11. *Board of Trade Inspectors Report*, op. cit.
12. B. Kirsch and C. Wolmar, 'Bergerland and the incredible story of London's very private landlords', *City Limits*, 13 January 1983, pp. 6–8.
13. According to a Parliamentary written answer dated 4 November 1983.
14. According to a Parliamentary written answer dated 29 November 1983.
15. Tony Levene, 'The family ties that bind a building society', *The Sunday Times*, 20 February 1983.
16. *Guide to Building Society Finance*, BSA, Second edition 1980, para. 1.41.
17. Tony Levene, op. cit.

9. Relations with other professionals

1. 'Home-loan men bite off more than their gums can chew', *The Economist*, 13 May 1983, pp. 85–86.
2. *Profits against Houses*, Consumer Development Project, Information and Intelligence Unit, 1976.
3. ibid.
4. ibid.
5. 'Watchdog', *Nationwide*, BBC 1, 17 May 1982.
6. *Profits against Houses* op. cit. pp. 50-51.
7. Reproduced in M. Boddy, *The Building Societies*, Macmillan 1980, p. 165.
8. ibid. p. 51
9. ibid. p. 52.
10. *The Guardian*, 20 May 1982.
11. 'Home-loan men bite off more then their gums can chew', op. cit.
12. *Profits against Houses*, op. cit. p. 57.

10. Fraud and other irregularities

1. Sir Herbert Ashworth, *The Building Society Story*, Franey & Co. 1980, p. 216.

2. *Report of the Chief Registrar of Friendly Societies for the year 1976*, Part 2, Building Societies, p. 20.
3. Ashworth, op. cit.
4. 'Grays Building Society' Investigation Under Section 110 of the Building Societies Act 1962. Report by Ian Hay-Davison and Murray Stuart-Smoth, HMSO, 1979.
5. ibid., p. 7.
6. ibid., p. 85.
7. ibid., p. 86.
8. ibid.
9. ibid., p. 88, the letter is reproduced in full.
10. ibid., p. 94, the letter is reproduced in full.
11. ibid., p. 162.
12. ibid., p. 163.
13. ibid., p. 164.
14. ibid., p. 165.
15. ibid.
16. ibid., p. 107
17. *Report of a Committee of Inquiry under the Joint Disciplinary Scheme concerning the Alfreton Building Society*, p. 22.
18. ibid., p. 23
19. ibid. pp. 28, 39
20. ibid., p. 2.
21. ibid., p. 38.
22. C. Moir, 'BSA blasts accountants', *The Sunday Telegraph*, 1982.
23. *Report of the Chief Registrar of Friendly Societies for the year 1979*, Part 2, Building Societies, p. 5.
24. Reported in *Building Societies Gazette*, June 1978, p. 586.
25. Reported in *Building Societies Gazette*, August 1981, p. 1010.
26. *Report of the Chief Registrar of Building Societies for the year 1974*, Part 2, Building Societies, p. 26.
27. 'Mortgage priority probe at London & South of England', *Building Societies Gazette*, April 1981, p. 394.
28. See for example, L.H. Leigh, *The Control of Commercial Fraud*, Heinemann 1982.
29. R. Garlick, 'The chink in the audit armour', *Accountants Weekly*, 21 April 1978, p. 10–11. The Provincial disputes some of the points in this article. In particular, they say they do not accept that all transactions assume some component of trust, and believe that adequate internal controls are built into their procedure, the audit department's duties being to verify that such controls exist. Personal communication, 15 March 1984.

11. Members *versus* directors

1. A. Nichols, *Management and Control in the Mutual Savings and Loan Associations*, Lexington, Mass.: Lexington Books 1972.
2. *The Guardian*, 24 February 1982.
3. 'Rebel shakes society to its foundations', *The Guardian*, 27 March 1982, p. 1.
4. 'Financial Notebook', *The Guardian*, 25 March 1983, p. 17.
5. ibid.
6. 'Rebel shakes society to its foundations', op. cit.
7. Committee to Review the Functioning of Financial Institutions, *Report*, Cmnd. 7937, HMSO 1980, para 905.
8. ibid., para 913.
9. Personal communication from Paul Twyman, 24 March 1984.

12. Proposals for reform

1. *Report of Chief Registrar of Friendly Societies 1981–1982*, pp. 16-21 particularly.
2. From 'Building societies end rate cartel', *Financial Times*, 22 October 1983, p. 30.
3. Parliamentary written answer, 19 December 1983.
4. Graham Turner, 'Nothing hasty about this movement', *Daily Telegraph*, 10 September 1983.
5. 'Home-loan bite off more than their gums can chew', *The Economist*, 13 May 1983, pp. 85–6.
6. ibid.
7. *Daily Mirror*, 6 October 1983, p. 7.
8. *The Future Constitution and Powers of Building Societies*, BSA 1983.
9. For example, *Building Society Accounts and Disclosure* Certified Accountants Publications 1983; and M. Boleat, *The Building Society Industry*, Allen & Unwin 1982.
10. Report of the Chief Registrar of Friendly Societies, Part 2, Building Societies, Appendix, 1978, pp. 38, 39.
11. See for example D.G. Mayes, *The Property Boom*, Martin Robertson 1979.